White Oblivion

A Novel
by Amirah Bellamy

White Oblivion

*is dedicated to the the fallen young heros of our time
that were brutally, savagely taken from this physical
realm and graciously welcomed into the ancestral and
spiritual realm.   May you enjoy your ascent to the
highest heights and your evolution into your true god
essence in immortal bliss….*

*Ashe…. Freddie Gray, Walter Scott, Anthony Hill, Akai
Gurley, Tami Rice, Victor White III, Dante Parker, Ezell
Ford, Michael Brown, Tyree Woodson, John Crawford
III, Eric Garner, Yvette Smith, Donitre Hamilton, Jordan
Baker, Barrington Williams, Carlos Alcis, Deion Fludd,
Jonathan Ferrell, Kimani Gray, Kyam Livingstone, Larry
Eugene Jackson, Jr., Miriam Carey, Tyrone West,
Chavis Carter, Dante Price, Duane Brown, Ervin
Jefferson, Jersey Green, Johnnie Kamahi Warren,
Justin Slipp, Kendrec McDade, Malissa Williams,
Nehemiah Dillard, Ramarley Graham, Raymond Allen,
Rekia Boyd, Reynaldo Cuevas, Robert Dumas Jr.,
Shantel Davis, Sharmel Edwards, Sgt. Mauel Loggins
Jr., Shereese Franci, Tamon Robinson, Timothy
Russell, Wendell Allen, Alonzo Ashley, Jimmell Cannon,
Kenneth Chamberlain, Kenneth Harding, Raheim
Brown, Reginald Doucet, Aaron Campbell, Alyana*

Jones, Danroy Henry, Derrick Jones, Steven Eugene Washington, Kiwane Carrington, Oscar Grant, Shem Walker, Victor Steen, Tarika Wilson, DeAunta Terrel Farrow, Sean Bell, Henry Glover, James Brisette, Ronald Madison,Timothy Stansbury, Alberta Spruill, Orlando Barlow, Ousmane Zongo, Michael Ellerbe, Timothy Thomas, Early Murray, Malcolm Ferguson, Patrick Dorismond, Prince Jones, Ronald Beasley, Amadou Diallo, Nicholas Heyward Jr., Malice Green, Edmund Perry, Eleanor Bumpurs, Michael Stewart, Ron Settles, Eula Love, Mark Clark, Fred Hampton & James Powell

Acknowledgments

I thank energy of Maat and my beautiful spirit guides who are always around me urging me on lovingly throughout my creative journey and inspiring me to realize more of who I truly am. I also thank my beautiful inspirational, creative soul group for keeping me humble.

1

I inhaled deeply taking in my first morning breath still gleaming from the night's glow. Enjoying the feeling of having been awakened by the beautiful song of the birds just outside my window I snuggled my head deeper into the nook of Doran's chest. After all of this time I still loved the feeling of mornings like this. I squeezed my eyes shutting them tighter and inhaled deeply again just to take in the goodness of the feeling with all of my senses. It was bliss.

I knew that Doran was my soul the day we saw one another and briefly exchanged words at Everlasting Life Cafe three years ago. Everlasting Life Cafe was a popular vegan restaurant in DC on Georgia Ave., N.W. that I went to maybe two to three times a year to treat myself. It was a bit pricy so I didn't go there often, but the food was absolutely delicious!

That day when I saw Doran he was looking breathtakingly gorgeous and so I struggled to maintain my composure trying not to gawk too much. He stood in line in front of me wearing a white t-shirt, blue sweatpants and black sneakers. I thought to myself, this man is a god!

Though externally everything about him was mediocre, he had an irresistible, strong magnetic energy that pulsated miles outward so much so that it swept me up off of my feet and hurled me into his outer space. I swear it was in his eyes.

Doran was a chocolate brown complexioned dream! He was average build and height and stood about 6'3. He wore his hair in a short close cut with a goatee. Though he seemed quite average to the passerby to me his aura was absolutely magical and I was instantly captivated by him. Yet it was the gaze of his eyes that I *felt* before I saw that drew me in for the kill. His eyes whispered to my soul requesting that I invite them in. Unable to resist their magnetic pull I obliged and looked back at them. Then once our eyes met it was an etheric explosion!

I could see that he felt it too because as he placed his order, ordering a couscous side, marinated mushrooms and a rising sun shake, he kept looking over at me as he spoke, seemingly a little distracted. Then once he completed his order and as if reading my mind he looked back at me and said "Peace goddess." In awe of the god before me I nodded and replied, "Peace god."

That was all that we said to one another, but it was a greeting that I never forgot. Then, surprisingly after placing his order and getting his food Doran left and I never saw him again until about 6 months later. We were both at Everlasting Life again. When I saw him again I thought to myself that it was just too good to be true.

That day I was there with my homegirl Cre. We were on our way home from a day of light shopping and both wanted to grab a bite to eat before heading in. We'd already stopped by Sweet Green where Cre had already picked up a salad, but I wasn't in the mood for salad so we also went to Everlasting Life, though it was a bit out of the way. I just had the most intense craving for their Garvey Burger so I sacrificed the extra gas and headed over to Everlasting Life to satisfy my craving.

"Girl I can't believe you drove all the way over here just to get that burger. Is that all you're ordering?" Cre asked.

"Yeah. It's the only thing I'm craving," I answered.

"Yeah, but damn girl if you drive all this way you may as well order something for later too. Aren't you at least gonna get a side?" Cre insisted.

"I guess you have a point. I'll go ahead and order some of their mac n cheese for later then. If I don't I'll beat myself later," I agreed.

Just as I walked up to order I felt it. It was that familiar stare. I didn't even have to look because I knew who it was.

"How may I help you today sis?" the waiter asked walking toward the counter where I was standing.

"Yes, I'd like to order ----" I began as my words trailed off.

The instant I felt it I became distracted by it and could barely even remember where I was, why I was there and most importantly what I wanted to order. Everything just went blank! I thought to myself, "Oh my

God!!! What the hell!" I quickly scrambled trying to remember what I wanted to order. I was so embarrassed!

"Oh my God I'm so sorry, but I forgot just that quick what I wanted to order. I must have gotten a brain freeze," I said jokingly trying to make light of my embarrassment.

"It's okay I understand. Happens to the best of us," the waiter said smiling.

"Oh yeah, I wanted to order a Garvey Burger and a small mac n cheese to go please," I said remembering again.

Cre looked over at me and snickered. She saw all of what was happening and I knew that I would hear about it once we left out of the restaurant.

Just then Doran came up to me and said, "Hello again goddess! It's a pleasant surprise seeing you again!"

In shock I quickly regained my composure after experiencing near paralysis of the mouth and replied, "Peace god. It's good to see you again also. How are you?"

"Well after seeing you I am well. How are you?" Doran responded.

"I'm well also," I answered.

I was so nervous that I had no idea what to say next. I didn't want things to end where they did last time and run the risk of never seeing him again so I wanted to come up with something to say to keep the conversation going, but I was frozen. Nervousness had taken me by the throat and I was paralyzed by it. This god was my soul and I had to stay connected to him this time. However, I didn't want to come off too desperate so I maintained my silence. I was so nervous that I stopped breathing. Noticing that I was holding my breath as I waited for my order I slowly inhaled then exhaled deeply trying to relax myself.

Seeing the calmness return to me Doran gazed into my eyes and spoke again, "So beautiful what are you getting into later?"

His gaze was so intense that it nearly made me hyperventilate. By then my nerves were shot! I had to get it together. This was my chance and I did *not* want to let him get away again.

"Just probably gonna hang out for a while at a friend's. Why do you ask?" I answered holding it together as best I could.

"Hoping that you'd like to share the time with me," Doran responded with a sexy smile that nearly made me lose my balance.

"Hmmm that could be a possibility," I replied smiling back at him.

"Well I'm a firm believer in making possibilities become realities so what do you say to us meeting back here at 7 o'clock this evening," he suggested.

His confidence, his sexiness and his peaceful demeanor had the butterflies in my stomach doing the cupid shuffle. There was just something so intriguing about him that grabbed me by the heart and made me melt at the mere sight of him.

By then I was so nervous that I could barely find the words to respond. I'd never experienced anything like that before. Usually I was so controlled, confident and sure of myself. I was a master at communication, but at that moment words had completely escaped me.

He stood gazing into my eyes with that hypnotic gaze of his patiently awaiting my response. My mind was racing. In fact, I felt as if I was outside of my mind and body looking on as an observer. Then the room went silent and everyone else disappeared.

Without any further hesitation I answered smiling back at him, "Yes, let's."

"Ok then I'll see you at 7 and enjoy your Garvey burger," he said grinning as he stepped up to the counter to place his order.

I was frozen in awe of the god before me, but I had to will myself to walk out of that restaurant. It helped to see Cre looking at me from the doorway grinning from ear to ear.

Once I made my way to her she said to me, "Wow! So that was *niiiice*... very nice."

"Whew! Girl let's go I need some air!" I said waving my hand to gesture for Cre to follow me out the door.

"So girl who was THAT?" Cre pryed.

"I don't even know, but I have a dinner date with him later," I said still in shock.

"What!?! Girl you didn't even get his name and you're having dinner with him later?" Cre asked.

"I know crazy right!" I said smiling at my own insanity.

I couldn't believe how badly I let my nerves get the better of me. Cre just looked at me and laughed as we headed out of the restaurant.

2

When Cre and I walked out of the restaurant what happened next sent my lovelorn thoughts of Doran to a screeching halt. As soon as we stepped outside of the restaurant doors there were two policemen, one black and one white, just a few steps away from the restaurant door who seemed to be giving the brothah that just walked out ahead of us a hard time.

"Sir we need to ask you a few questions," the white cop began.

"Yeah and its best that you cooperate," the black cop added already acting a bit high-strung.

Looking at them skeptically the brothah replied, "I don't think you have the right to question me about anything. I'm pretty sure I haven't been involved in anything that would warrant the police needin to ask me any questions. All I was just tryin to do was grab a bite to eat before heading home."

Soon Doran, like us, and some others had come outside and stopped to see what was going on. We were all looking on to see what the policemen were up to.

Then the white cop said "Sir you need to cooperate. Now we can either do this here or down at the station. All we want to do is ask you a few questions sir."

Getting a lot more agitated, the brothah responded saying, "Like I said I ain't done nothing that would warrant ya'll needin to ask me nothing. Now am I under arrest or not? If not, I got nothing else to say to you and I'm going home."

By then a crowd was forming and so the black cop started waving his hand around motioning for everyone to leave saying, "People keep it moving. This does not concern you and there's nothing for you to see."

Someone from the crowd yelled, "Yeah right! We aint' goin nowhere. The minute we do we gon hear about how this brothah died for so-called *resisting* arrest!"

Then a sistah yelled, "Yeah! So whatever ya'll gon do you gon do it with a dozen witnesses! We ain't goin nowhere and you can't take us all in for that!"

Everyone stood firm and not a soul moved. That seemed to have given the brothah being harassed some solace because he maintained that he was not going anywhere with the police and that he didn't have anything to say to them.

"You can't make me say nothin to you! If I say anything to you its on my own free will. Ya'll ain't gon never take my free will away from me! So it's best ya'll go on an leave me be," the brothah continued getting more agitated.

Tensions were mounting and I could feel that things were about to take a turn for the worse. Then just as I predicted moments later as the brothah went to turn to walk away clutching his bag of food tighter the overzealous white cop overreacted by jumping and lunging at the brothah grabbing him by the arm and yanking it behind him saying, "Sir that's it! We're taking you in."

Following the white cop's lead, the black cop grabbed the brothah's other arm that had the bag of food in it. However, because he had yanked the brothah's arm so forcefully it sent the bag of food flying up in the air. When the food descended it landed on the black cop's head. He yelled out in pain as the food was piping hot having just been prepared in the restaurant. More than that it looked like one items in the bag was soup, which was no doubt boiling hot.

The black cop grew angrier and was by then quite embarrassed and began to take it out on the brothah yanking out his cuffs, handcuffing the brothah then roughing him up as they made their way around the corner to the police car.

The crowd started to grow in size and increasingly more agitated as people began shouting at the cops saying that they had better let the brothah go, urging them to stop harassing black people. Then we all followed the cops around the corner and some had even pulled out their cellphones and began recording.

The closer the three men got to the car the more the brothah struggled to break free. We all looked on empathetically as we felt his angst in not wanting to get into the police car.

Tensions were very high surrounding such matters as several black boys had been murdered while in police custody over the past year or so. Too many times brothahs had been taken away in those cars never to be seen alive again.

So by the time they were within a few feet of the car the brothah began to yell emphatically, "Man you're hurtin me! I ain't resistin! You ain't got nothin on me! What you takin me in for!"

Then seemingly having reached his boiling point the black cop faked a scuffle, forced the brothah to the ground and began kicking him viciously joined in by the white cop. They were kicking the brothah with such zeal that some of the brothahs standing by began to yell threats to the cops telling them to stop or they were gonna stop them.

Then , seeing that they were outnumbered and after hearing what was being said, the white cop stopped kicking the brothah, turned and drew his gun waving it at the crowd yelling, "Now back up. This does not concern you. This is police business. If you all don't go on home we'll take you all in for obstruction."

"For obstructing what pig! Obstructing you from unjustly whipping that brothah's ass! He said he ain't resisting and the minute he said that you went to whippin on him like he stole on you. You got him in cuffs so ain't no way he can fight you *or* resist," A brothah from the crowd yelled.

"Yeah!" another yelled. "We ain't going a gotdamn place!"

By then the white cop was calling for backup and in what seemed like seconds the place was swarming with cops. They were like parasites the way they so quickly multiplied.

As more cops arrived they began to make the ever expanding crowd disperse. There were by then so many people that I had lost track of Doran.

As the crowd began to disperse Cre and I decided to head on home both reeling from what we had just witnessed.

Over the past year at least 10 black boys had been unjustly brutally murdered by cops and so the black community was fed up to say the least. Scenes like that were becoming more and more common and it was beginning to feel like we were going backwards in time, reliving the civil rights era.

As the mother of a young, male child my heart always went out to the mothers of the fallen boys. I couldn't imagine how painful that must have been to live through. It was a horrifying thought.

Then briefly thinking about Doran I wondered how I would have responded if that was him the cops were harassing. It easily could have been him about 2 minutes later. I shuttered at the thought.

Then looking forward to my date with him scheduled for later that evening I was sure that what just happened would be the main topic of discussion. Nonetheless, I looked forward to seeing him later as I made my way home still pondering the day's eery events.

As planned, I returned to Everlasting Life that evening to have dinner with Doran. He was everything I expected and more. I was so smitten by his intelligence. He really had an insightful perspective on the whole cop brutality issue, which we of course discussed at length for much of the night.

As expected Doran was deeply insightful on a number of subjects and for me it seemed that he and I were a match made in heaven. I'd never felt that before. Yet that's the effect that Doran had on me even to the present day. So from that day forward Doran and I had been inseparable and were married six months later.

3

As I lay reminiscing on the blissful memories of him I snuggled up as close to Doran as I could get. He was sleeping so soundly and peacefully. I could feel the gentle beating of his heart as I lay wrapped in his arms on his chest. Being with Doran was the most satisfying part of my life. On mornings like that I just wanted to lay in his arms forever.

It was Sunday morning, which was the one day that I got to sleep in. I had a yoga studio on Capitol Hill in downtown D.C. on 8th Street and normally had to get up at the crack of dawn on weekday mornings to get to the studio in time for my 5:30am sunrise yoga sessions. Yet, on Sundays I got to sleep in so lying there with Doran all those years later still made me giddy. I never wanted those mornings to end.

I never figured out what it was about Doran that made me so crazy about him, but whatever it was had me feeling like a lovesick schoolgirl ever since the day I met him. It was three years later and I still got butterflies in my stomach whenever I saw him or whenever he would call. Though he was my husband, from the way that I acted with him onlookers would often think that we'd just started courting.

To the present day when Doran would look at me it send chills up and down my spine. He would touch me and I would still melt. He'd smile at me and I'd still blush. I was smitten with him and anyone could see it.

I started to see the sun's glow outside my eyelids so I opened my eyes imagining it's warmth caressing my skin. Doran rubbed my arms apparently waking up as well. I looked up at him as he was beginning to awaken, or so I thought. To my surprise, he was merely repositioning himself still seemingly in deep sleep. I decided to close my eyes again and continued to enjoy the bliss of lying in his arms.

Within minutes I had dozed back off and was again sleeping peacefully when all of a sudden out of nowhere I felt a sharp tug. Startled I sprung straight up.

"Doran! What's wrong?" I asked reaching over to grab his arm thinking that he was having a nightmare and had accidentally tugged me.

"Who the hell are you?" Doran yelled yanking away from me and jumping out of the bed looking at me as if I was a complete stranger.

Doran looked almost terrified staring down at me. I wondered if he was having some kind of psychotic break, at least until I saw what he saw.

4

The look in Doran's eyes startled me so I looked to see what about me was so startling to him. When I looked I couldn't believe my eyes! Immediately I jumped up and ran to the bathroom mirror to see if I was seeing what I thought I was seeing. As I looked at the face staring back at me I was sure that I had either lost my mind or that I was a part of someone's cruel joke.

Meanwhile, Doran came running after me still yelling at me and asking who the hell I was. My mind was racing and I couldn't answer him. I had no idea.

Trying to calm myself and Doran I found the will speak.

"It's me Doran," I said.

"Me who? Who the hell are you? Where did you come from? How did you get in my bed and where is my wife!?!" he yelled.

"Baby it's me. I'm Netty. I don't know what happened. I don't know why I look like this, but I promise you it's me baby," I reasoned.

"Baby? Don't call me that. I don't know you! How do you know my wife and where is she?" Doran said beginning to cover himself with a nearby towel.

"Baby I swear I'm just as confused about this as you are. It's really me, Netty!" I said beginning to tear up.

I was scared out of my wits by then. I couldn't figure out what was going on. I didn't know if I was in some alternate universe or what. It seemed that one minute I was in heaven and the next I was in a living hell. I was truly in a living nightmare. The question buzzing like a siren in my head was how was this possible? How did I go to sleep as one person and wake up as another? Then not only did I wake up as another person, but I woke up as a white woman!

Doran was furious and he wasn't listening to anything that I had to say. I was struggling to deal with my own terror while trying to calm him down and reassure him of who I was, but it didn't do a bit of good. He started pacing back and forth. I'd never seen him so angry. In fact, I'd never seen him angry at all. He always had such a peaceful disposition.

I started to get worried that things might take a turn for the worst so I decided to say something to assure Doran that I was telling the truth. I needed to calm him down so I could try to figure out what was going on with me.

"I could go for a Garvey Burger right about now," I said looking over at Doran hoping for a sign that he'd realize that I was still me.

"What did you say?" Doran said freezing in his tracks moving toward me.

"I'm just trying to get you to see that it's me baby," I reasoned.

"Look I don't know who the hell you are, but you got about 3 seconds to get the hell up outta my house!" Doran exclaimed sounding more threatening.

"Baby look I'm scared to death here and I'm doing my best to hold it together. I'm just as confused as you are. I feel like me. I sound like me, but I damn sure don't look like myself. I don't know what the hell happened as I slept. I wish you would calm down so that we can figure this out together. I need you baby I'm scared," I pouted before continuing. "Look, so that we can at least move past you believing me please ask me anything and I promise I'll answer it to prove that I'm me. Really baby ask me anything, something that only I'd know," I reasoned.

He looked at me intently as if pondering what to ask me. Then he said, "What show did I used to watch with my grandfather before he died when I was 8 years old?"

"Andy Griffith," I answered confidently.

He paused for a moment as if in shock then moments later he ran over to me and grabbed ahold of me holding me tight.

"It *is* you!" Doran said matter-of-factly.

"Yes it is, but I have no idea what or how this happened. Everything about me feels the same. How could this have happened baby? Is it permanent?" I asked wanting Doran to have the answers.

"I've never heard of anything like this baby. Did you feel okay when you went to bed last night?" Doran asked.

"I felt fine and I still do now. I don't think it's a disease or anything. I mean look at me baby. I don't look sick. I'm just white!" I said startled as I looked at myself in the mirror again.

It was difficult to look. I was a white woman. My once henna-coated kinky, curly tresses had become straight, stringy, reddish brunette strands that hung to the middle of my back. My once caramel-coated melanated brown skin was a pale bleached ghostly skin suit. Even the texture of it was different. It had a more clammy texture. My scent was different also. I couldn't pinpoint what it was, but something about it was very different. Also, my once thick beautiful lips were thin and barely visible. My life-giving hips and thighs were instead and extension of my back. It seemed that even the air that I breathed had changed though I knew that part was only in my head. I just detested the face staring back at me in the mirror. Who was she and why had she taken over my body!

Both Doran and I just stood gazing at her, our thoughts racing a million miles per minute. We had so many unanswered questions. She would have to give us some answers.

Doran gazed into her eyes and said, "Well your eyes are still the same. Those I know."

"Really? Everything just seems so foreign to me at this point. The only thing that I recognize is me from the inside. I still *feel* black. Does my voice still sound the same? It does to me," I said.

"It's got a bit of a higher pitch. Try to sing something," Doran suggested.

Among my many crafts I was also a singer. I sang a quick jazz riff and from the look on Doran's face it seemed that my vocals were still in tact. I did a yoga pose to see if I still had my flexibility. I did reverse triangle pose with ease and concluded that my flexibility was also still in tact.

"I know this sounds crazy but can you log onto the computer babe and look online to see if you can find anything about this. Maybe it's happened to someone else," I proposed.

"I highly doubt that, but we can look," Doran said heading back to our bedside table and grabbing his Macbook Air as he made his way to sit on his side of the bed.

He started typing in search terms like 'waking up a different person' and 'waking up in a different reality.' Mostly what he found pertained to coma patients who woke up speaking different languages. As for the latter search term the only thing that came up was someone talking about out-of-body experiences. There wasn't a single case of anyone waking up appearing to be a completely different person.

I started to panic. What if this was permanent. How would I live that way. I couldn't be her. I loved me and I wanted my own body back. Besides that everyone in the conscious community knew me as a black woman. Then I hadn't even thought about how my kids would react!

"Babe how are we gonna explain this to Ina when she wakes up?!?!" I said nearly hyperventilating at the thought.

"I haven't thought that far ahead. I'm still trying to digest this myself," Doran said looking at me with a hint of disgust.

Doran was by no means into white girls and I could only imagine how repulsed he must have been feeling. He was a brother that truly loved the sistahs. Besides that he was a very conscious brothah and deeply metaphysical. He believed in all things melanated so I knew that what was happening had to be blowing his mind. I knew that he would need time to digest it all so I made my way back to the bathroom to give him a moment.

When I got to the bathroom I looked at her again in the mirror.

"Who are you?" I asked her aloud.

There was no reply so I asked again.

"Who are you? Tell me what you want from me. Why me?" I asked hoping to get a response.

Still nothing.

I decided to take in some deep breaths to try to calm myself down so that maybe I could hear a response. I thought that perhaps I just had too much mind chatter going on with all the excitement of the morning's events.

"Who are you?" I asked again after quieting my thoughts a bit.

I still got no response.

"Get out! Give me my body back! Give it back now!" I began screaming at the mirror.

The more I looked at her the more enraged I became. I hated her. I had to find a way to get rid of her. I began screaming and crying uncontrollably and Doran came running into the bathroom to see what was wrong. I had started scratching my skin. I thought that maybe it would come off and that it was a cruel joke. My nails were long and had broken the skin so blood was everywhere. Doran ran in and grabbed my hands to stop me.

"Netty stop! Look what you're doing. Stop this. This isn't helping. You have to calm down so we can figure this out," Doran consoled.

"Who are you?!?!!" I continued to yell louder.

"She is you baby and we will deal with this," Doran said holding me in his arms.

As he held me the tears began to fall down my face like waterfalls. I cried out as if in pain. It was devastating. It was horrific and what I felt was the worst possible thing imaginable. Never in a million years did I think that I could look at myself with such disdain. Yet at that moment I hated myself to the very depths of me and I hated that I did.

I wept in Doran's arms for what seemed like an eternity. He patiently held me close and allowed me to cry until I had no more tears. For me it was as if someone had died. Then I guess in a way someone did, me. The imposter that stared back at me in the mirror had taken my place. As I gazed into Doran's eyes weakened by what seemed like hours of crying I could also see that he felt the same way. I could see that he wanted Netty back. No matter how strong he tried to be for me the truth was still in his eyes. Doran's eyes always told the story of what went on inside of him and so I knew for us the journey was just beginning.

"So what now? I can't stay in this room forever. How am I supposed to live like this. How are we supposed to live like this? I can see in your eyes that I repulse you and I get it because I can't even bear to look at myself. I feel like this is it for me. My life is over. I can't go to the studio like this. I can't let Ina see me like this. Then what about J? What are we gonna tell him when he comes home? I can't hold him off forever," I rambled.

Ina was our 10-year-old daughter and J was our 22-year-old son who was away at a college in Colorado completing his final year. Doran didn't have children when I met him, but quickly fell right into a father role to both of my children fully claiming them both as his own. He didn't believe in step-children so we always referred to them as our children and Doran fit right into our family as if he had been there all along.

"Try not to worry about all of these things right now. We're not going to figure anything out with you being so upset. Try to calm down first okay," Doran said still holding me trying to calm me.

I had cried so much and gotten myself so worked up that I had exhausted myself and as Doran stroked my head I began to doze off.

5

When I woke up it was near noon. I must have worn myself out after having gotten so upset. I looked up and Doran was sitting on the bed staring at me.

"I know that I repulse you" I said looking down.

"No you don't. This is difficult for both of us. You're still you and I can still see your light shining through and that will never repulse me," Doran said assuringly.

I couldn't believe that Doran was taking this all so well. Though I knew that a big part of it was that he was just trying to be strong for me. I was clearly falling apart. Normally I was one of the most confident, uplifting people anyone would ever want to know. Though after waking up in someone else's body with no explanation as to how it happened I was a wreck.

I heard what Doran said, but I had no idea how or if I would ever get through such a horrifying experience. Nonetheless, I did feel some solace from Doran. He was doing everything in his power to quell my fears and for that I was grateful. It was one of the many things that I loved about him.

"I know... you're right babe, but I swear even in knowing that, I'm still very much devastated by this whole thing. This isn't exactly the type of thing that you just figure out a quick solution for. I mean I AM IN SOMEBODY ELSE'S BODY!" I exclaimed getting worked up again.

"Yes you're right... you are... and true neither of us has any idea as to how we're going to work our way through this. At the same time if this is who you are now I will love you the same because I know that you're still you. You're still the same woman that I fell deeply in love with 3 years ago. You're still the same woman that I am so proud to call mine. You're still the same woman that makes my life complete. I don't care what you look like baby. Nothing will change that. So if you don't know already I'm in this with you. We'll face this together. We'll work through this and I mean that. There has to be an explanation and a way to deal with it," Doran said endearingly.

"*Deal* with it? You mean fix me right? I see how you look at me now. I know that you love me, but I repulse you right now. I see it in your eyes. I hear what you *say*, but I also see what I see. I repulse myself right now so I can understand," I sulked.

On that note, Doran walked out of the room. I knew that I had pushed too hard. I didn't know what else to do but to push him away. I was the one trapped in someone else's body and he would never truly understand that in a million years.

I sat on the bed sulking and feeling sorry for myself. I knew that it wouldn't do any good, but I just needed a moment to be broken. I needed some time alone to fall apart and I was glad that Doran had left the room so that I had time to do just that. I must have wept until I had no tears left. The pain in my heart pierced me to the core. I couldn't figure out a way to feel better and to be okay with what was happening. The only thing that I knew how to do was to embrace the pain and it hurt like hell.

I ended up staying holed up in our room for 3 days! I just wasn't ready to face the world as *her*. She disgusted me. So for 3 days I slept, cried, sulked and then slept some more. After a while I didn't even notice that Doran was even there. I didn't care about anything anymore. I felt like my life had ended and I wasn't about to give her the benefit of having a life when mine had so abruptly been taken from me.

Then, on the afternoon of the third day I got up and went to the bathroom to look at her again. She was an abomination. I hated everything about her. Who was she? Where did she come from and why me? Why on earth did she choose me? There had to be *some* explanation as to why. I had to figure the whole thing out. There just *had* to be some explanation. Doran was right. The more I sat with myself the more I began to see the truth in what Doran had said. I had to somehow manage to pull myself together enough to figure this all out. I sat up on the bed, wiped my tears, closed my eyes and began to take some deep breaths.

I thought to myself, "At least I'm alive. I'm still here so that means there must be a way out of this. This must be some sort of test of my will."

As a yogi I knew well of seeing the better side of things. I had to snap out of this funk and get myself together. I quickly jumped up and went to hop into the shower. I undressed and was about to throw on a shower cap when I realized that with my new hair there was no need for that. I wore my hair natural and so I was used to having a head full of thick, nappy kinks to protect whenever I took a shower to save myself from having to detangle it afterwards. So not having my own hair would take some getting used to. Hair was such a huge part of my life. I attributed much of my beauty to my hair, which I had taken great pains to grow over the years. My curly, kinky tresses were near hip length and I hated the fact that they were no longer there.

Nonetheless, I maintained my intentions on focusing my energy on figuring out my dilemma. I had to redirect my focus away from what I didn't have and direct it onto what I did have. I also had to focus on learning more about what was happening.

As I stepped into the shower I nearly cringed after seeing the pale, white leg. I needed some serious sun! My skin looked like death. After getting into the shower I looked down at my breast. I'd never seen nipples so pink. My skin texture even felt different. It was a lot smoother and being in the shower gave it even more of a slip.

I closed my eyes and immersed my face into the water stream. I wished that I could wash it all away. I wished that when I opened my eyes I would once again be my true self. Then I had a thought. Perhaps this *was* my true self. Was I living a dream all along? Was I finally waking up from a dream? I pondered those thoughts for a few minutes as I lost myself in the stream of the water flowing down my pale, white skin and stringy hair. Just then Doran came into the bathroom.

"Wow! Glad to see you moving around a little," he said clearly struggling to sound cheery. He looked exhausted. It was clear that he hadn't been getting much sleep. He was no doubt up worrying about me.

"Yeah, I can't sulk forever. Besides that I have to figure this thing out so I decided to start by getting cleaned up. I have lots of work to do. Is Ina awake yet?" I queried.

"Yeah, she and I were downstairs eating a bowl of cereal. I told her that I had something to discuss with her. I figured that I needed to give her a heads up on what was going on with you so that she wouldn't be in too much shock when she saw you. Besides that she's been asking about you and getting really worried. So whenever you're ready she's ready to see you. Feel free to take your time though baby because I know that this is very difficult for you. We just have to take it all in stride," Doran said talking to me from the other side of the shower curtain.

"Ok thanks for doing that and taking care of things the past few days. I owe you! Soooo I guess I'll go see her when I get dressed. I have to face the world sooner or later, but what are we gonna to tell everyone else? Have you figured that out yet?" I asked Doran hoping that he had some good suggestions.

"No I haven't quite figured that out yet, but I do think that for now we should just keep this within the family. As for the studio you can come up with a fake name and say that you're a fill-in instructor until you, well the real you, gets back. What do you think abou that?" Doran asked.

"I think that's a perfect solution. That'll give us some time to figure this all out. Thanks for that," I said graciously.

I was so glad that Doran was taking on so much of the weight of this issue for me because I had truly fallen apart and was only beginning to pick up the pieces. I had not a clue as to what I was going to do about this long term. I did, however, wonder how this would affect my marriage. Would Doran want to be seen with me in public now? I decided to just ask him. We always had a very honest, open relationship.

"So babe how are you going to feel about being seen out in public with me now? I mean in the conscious community and even among your own friends its sure to raise more than a few eyebrows. How are you going to deal with that?" I asked as I stepped out of the shower seeing Doran sitting on the top toilet seat lid deep in thought.

Looking at me a little startled he answered, "Baby we will take it all in stride. I'll be fine. I know that you're still you. I think the difficult part will be getting used to the stares. I'll just have to prepare for that emotionally as will you. The question is are *you* ready for that? I'll have to be since this is our reality now. I've never dated a white girl before so this should be interesting. At least I got me a cool white girl though," Doran said jokingly trying to lighten the mood.

"Babe, I'm not a white girl. Please don't call me that," I fussed.

"Yeah well I'm looking at you right now and you sure look like a white girl to me. Damn baby what happened to your ass? Oh no, not my creamy thighs! They're gone too! Now THAT might be a problem," Doran said joking.

"Come on babe I feel bad enough," I pouted.

"I know, but you know what they say about once you go black," Doran said laughing. "I can definitely see why they say that now. Ya'll white girls just don't cut it for me, but it's okay baby cause I still remember when. I still even have my pictures of when. Good thing I documented it before this happened. I'll just visualize when I look at you. If I keep doing that that's what I'll see," Doran said.

"Really babe, really!" I snapped.

"Well I see that your black girl attitude is still the same," Doran said laughing.

"That's okay, keep it up and you really will be having to remember when with those pictures of yours," I said.

Doran was a photographer and one of the best. He shot everyone from celebrities to well-known politicians. He had accumulated several dozens of photo shoots of me over the years. So he figured that if all else failed he could always look at them to remember what I looked like. I was already missing my old body terribly and thought I would need to see some of those pictures myself.

Doran jumped into the shower after I got out so I went to get dressed. After getting dressed I came back into the bathroom to figure out what to do with my new hair. I couldn't bear the sight of the lifeless look of it so I just put it up into a bun. I could see that the hair thing was really going to be quite an adjustment for me.

6

Once Doran got out of the shower and got dressed he and I headed downstairs to present the imposter me to Ina. She was sitting in the living room on the loveseat reading a book. She was an avid reader and spent more time reading than most kids spent playing video games. It was one of the many things that I absolutely loved about her. Both she and Doran loved reading. It was actually how the two of them bonded initially. They would sit on the couch together both deeply engrossed in their book of choice sitting as quiet as church mice.

Doran decided to dive right in without delay and greeted Ina as I trailed closely behind him. "Good afternoon again Ina! Here she is! Presenting your new mom!" he said flagging his hand in front of me like he was Bob Barker on the Price Is Right and Ina was getting a new car.

"Oh wow! Is this real?" Ina gasped in utter shock.

"Yeah it's real. Touch her. She's real alright," Doran said.

Frozen and apparently glued to her seat Ina said, "Wow mom is that really you in there? How did this happen? I had no idea this was possible. Are you going to get your old self back? How will you explain this to everyone? How do I explain it to my friends? How will you teach classes at the studio?"

Ina was full of questions and she bombarded me with each and every one of them.

"I know Ina this is quite a shock to us all. For now we're just gonna keep this to ourselves so no one will be telling anyone outside of here. I'll tell J myself so he won't be startled when he comes home," I explained.

"Can I touch it mom?" Ina asked.

"Sure," I said as Ina slowly made her way towards me as if she was approaching a haunted house on Halloween.

She inched toward me standing just inches away and touched my hand, then moved her hand up my arm and lastly touched my hair.

"Oh my god mom this isn't real. Are you gonna be like this forever? Will you ever come back to us? I can't imagine having a white mom," Ina said.

"Ina I'm still me and you don't have a white mom. I hope that you can see that," I said.

"Yes Ina you'll see soon enough that in every other way she's still very much your mom. Just say something to tick her off and you'll quickly find out," Doran chimed in.

"Alright now I told you about that babe. Don't start it," I snapped.

"See, I told you," Doran said laughing.

"I'm glad you find this so amusing. Just wait until you wake up as a white man in the morning. We'll see how funny it is then," I said.

"Well when I do I'll just make the best of it and get all the things that I was denied as a black man. Shoot, I'll probably get paid 3 times as much! Maybe that won't be half bad. So how do I make that happen baby? Give it to me step by step," Doran joked.

"Dad this is serious. How can you joke at a time like this? How are we gonna get mom back?" Ina said looking very concerned.

"He's just trying to lighten the mood a bit Ina. This is difficult for all of us, but we're working on fixing it," I said assuringly giving her a hug.

"I'm really worried about you mom. This is really serious," Ina said sounding 10 years older than she was.

We all headed over to the couch to discuss things further. We had a huge oversized brown couch where I sat between Ina and Doran. Ina sat still staring at me in shock. She looked at me like I was a science project gone wrong. Meanwhile, Doran tried not to stare, but he couldn't hide it very well because it was written all over his face. I started to feel like a contagious disease.

"Baby I can see that we're making you feel uncomfortable and we really don't mean to. It's just going to take some getting used to seeing you in this body. We know you're still you and we still love you," Doran said apparently sensing my discomfort.

"I know babe. It's just hard seeing my family look at me like I'm an alien," I said.

"So let's discuss this. We have no idea how or why this happened. We don't know how long it will last. In the meantime we each have to continue living our lives. So where do we go from here?" Doran asked Ina and I.

"I guess we continue to live as we always have while we try to make sense of it all and look for a solution," I said.

"Yeah dad I guess you're right, but mom I'm sorry this happened to you. I wish I could fix it for you," Ina said.

"I wish you could too baby. I know this is difficult for you too. Imagine how I felt when I first looked in the mirror and how I still feel everytime I look in the mirror and see this face," I said.

"So babe I do have one question for you. Can you still dance?" Doran said laughing.

"What!?! No you didn't! Of course I can!" I snapped.

"Ha ha! I told you she was still black!" Doran roared.

"Are you sure mom? Cause if you can't how are you going to teach your classes where you need rhythm?" Ina asked.

"Ina, don't you start too! I told ya'll I'm still black! Put on some music and I'll prove it! Ya'll are gonna find out!" I said.

"Alright, let's find out," Doran said reaching for his phone to find us some tunes. He scrolled through his playlist and put on some Nas.

At first I nodded my head to the beat, then I slowly got up and started to dance. As soon as I started dancing Doran and Ina roared with laughter.

"What is so funny!" I asked as I stopped dancing.

"Sorry mom, but we're just not used to seeing you dance as a white woman. You can really dance too," Ina said trying to placate me.

"Yeah baby we're not laughing to make fun of you. We're laughing with you. We're having fun with you baby," Doran added.

"Ok if you say so, but ya'll gotta stop laughing at me though every time I do something "black" so to speak," I said.

I was glad to have them both to go through this with me. I don't know what I would have done if I didn't have them and their bringing humor to such a traumatic situation was exactly what I needed. They really did lessen the sting of it all for me.

"So babe let's go out," Doran said.

"What?" I said looking over at him shocked by his question.

"Yeah, let's go out. You're gonna have to go out soon enough so we may as well do it now. You've got to get used to this body. In fact, we all do. So let's do it. Let's all go out right now," Doran persisted.

I sat on the couch pondering his proposition.

"Mom, Dad is right. Let's go out. We all have to get used to your new body," Ina chimed in.

Ina chiming in really pulled at my heart strings so I stood up and said, "Ok let's go."

"Yaaay!" Ina screeched.

Doran reached over and hugged me.

"I'm so glad that you're willing to take this step baby. You're really being brave through all of this. I'm so proud of you," Doran said smiling at me.

7

Since we were all hungry we decided to go to a restaurant and grab a bite to eat. We went to a mutual favorite, a little Thai restaurant in Capitol Hill on Pennsylvania Avenue near my studio. The restaurant was so tiny that it was hardly noticeable and was never crowded, but the food was absolutely delicious. We figured it would be a good way to ease into things since there likely wouldn't be very many people dining there at that time.

Getting there was uneventful, though we hadn't travelled very far to get there. We lived just about 15 minutes away in a newly renovated row house off of 13th and Irving Streets N.W. D.C..

Our renovated home was a dream. We bought the house dirt cheap as it was in shambles when we bought it. Then, we basically gutted it and Doran and some friends of his did all of the renovations.

There were cherry hardwood floors throughout. We were actually able to keep much of the original hardwood floors, which was a plus.

There were 2 levels and a full basement, which we made into a basement apartment for J. The basement apartment was complete with 1 master suite bedroom, which had a full bath. There was also a half bath off of the living room area. There was a beautiful eat-in kitchen which I had the time of my life designing. We put a lot into designing it figuring that when J moved out permanently we could rent it out. Basement apartment rentals went for a nice amount in DC.

On the first floor toward the back side of the house Doran put in a beautiful gourmet chef's kitchen for me. There was also a half bath just off of the kitchen leading up toward the living room. The living room was done in the style of a great room so the kitchen fed right into it. We weren't the formal type so I requested it be designed that way as I didn't see a need for a formal living room.

Then on the second floor were 3 bedrooms including our master suite. I designed Ina's room with all the girly bells and whistles. So it was designed with all things pinkalicious. She loved it. She had a beautiful full-sized canopy bed, a computer desk, a 40-inch wall mounted flat screen tv, a 3-story black barbie house, a toy box filled every little girl's dream toys and a huge bookshelf filled to capacity.

Next to Ina's room was the yoga/meditation room. It was our sacred space where we had an altar set up. My crystal collection was also displayed there along with several other sacred items that each of us had contributed.

Then on the other side of the meditation room was our master suite. I decorated it in a modern zen minimalist design, as was much of our house. I did it that way because I wanted it to be reminiscent of a spa retreat. So imagine heaven in a bedroom and that was our master suite.

Our king-size bed had a padded leather headboard and the fluffiest, most luxurious bedding that I could find. We had one large marble-top dresser and a huge walk-in closet in which Doran and I split it half. Doran needed just as much space as I did for all of his photography equipment. On each side of the bed were two end tables.

For me our home was a piece of heaven and under the current set of circumstances I dreaded the thought of leaving that heaven to go out into the world with this white skin.

As I sat on the edge of our bed putting on my socks my nerves had started to get the best of me. By the time we made it out the front door I was a wreck. Our neighborhood was predominantly black and so I think in large part I feared being judged by them. I really felt for Doran, though he didn't seem at all concerned with the stares that would undoubtedly come as a result of our newly interracial relationship.

Nonetheless, Doran suggested that we go ahead and dive into this thing and deal with the challenges of it as they came. Though I agreed with him I wasn't sure that I was emotionally ready to go through with it. Yet, despite my apprehension I went ahead and did as Doran suggested and dove in.

Since it was a weekday afternoon parking was tricky. However, we lucked up and Doran got a space right in front of the restaurant. I was relieved because that meant I wouldn't have to endure what I knew would be a terrifying walk down the street.

I hopped out of the car and nearly ran Ina and Doran over running into the restaurant. Thankfully it was Fall so I was able to take every precaution in disguising myself, wearing a hat, long sleeves and long pants. So my mad dash into the restaurant was sheer paranoia.

I don't know why I was disguising myself because no one else around knew or had ever seen me. I guess it was more about my feeling a sense of shame in my new skin.

When we went into the restaurant we were seated immediately. The restaurant was fairly empty and besides us there was only one couple there. They were a cute little white elderly couple sitting a couple tables away from where we were seated.

Though I felt really self conscious of my new skin it seemed that no one else in the restaurant cared because no one even gave us a second look as we headed over to our table.

I already knew what I wanted to order so I didn't even need to look over the menu. I wanted the vegetarian red curry. Doran and Ina said they wanted to try something new so they were intently looking over the menu before ordering.

The waitress, a tiny Thai woman who looked to be middle aged brushed over to our table in what seemed like less than a minute after we were seated.

"Hi, can I take yo orda?" she asked in a thick accent.

"Not yet we need a little more time thanks," Doran said with a hint of agitation.

He hated being rushed. As much as I loved Asian food Doran only took me to Asian restaurants to appease me. He hated how they always seemed to hurry us to get in and get out. He said that he didn't appreciate being herded like cattle through a restaurant.

I looked up at Doran and smiled. He knew that my smile was in reference to how short he was with the waitress.

"I don't know why after all these years of doing business in this country they don't have better customer service," Doran said.

"Baby I just think it's cultural. I don't think they mean to be rude," I suggested.

"Culture or not. The culture here is to not be rude where people are spending their hard earned money in your establishment," Doran snapped.

"That's true. Maybe someday that miracle will happen," I said with a hint of sarcasm.

"So Ina what are you ordering?" Doran asked.

Still looking a bit uncertain Ina said, "I think I want the fried rice again dad."

"I thought you were gonna try something new. What about trying the pad Thai tofu? It's usually very good and I think you'll like it," Doran suggested.

"Yeah I agree. You'll probably like that one Ina," I added.

"Hmmmm. Well okay I'll try it," Ina hesitated.

"Good. I'm gonna try this dish called Panang Jae," Doran said struggling to pronounce it correctly.

"Let me see that one," I said picking up my menu. "Ummmm looks good baby. Sounds like it's a lot like the vegetarian red curry."

"Yeah I know. It's at least an attempt to order something different though so give me *some* credit," Doran replied in response to my indirect jab.

"I know and I'm proud of you babe," I said in an attempt to smooth things over.

The waitress returned and that time we were ready to order. Doran ordered for everyone, the waitress took our menus and we all sat in awkward silence while we waited.

"So how are you doing? It's not so bad right?" Doran asked breaking the silence.

"I guess not. At least there aren't many people here," I said relieved.

"Yeah I figured we should ease into things. I didn't want to make you feel too stressed," Doran added.

"I wonder how it will be when you take me to school though mom. I mean school *is* still open tomorrow," Ina said sounding concerned.

"I know and I've been thinking about that. Babe can't you continue taking her just for a while until we figure out what our cover story is going to be?" I asked.

"Hmmm. I'll do it, but just for this week. I don't want to put this off for too long. We can't let this thing take over our lives by prolonging the inevitable," Doran answered.

"I know babe, but this is really hard for me and I'm dealing with it as best I can. I just don't want to be overwhelmed," I said.

"I'm not going to overwhelm you, but I also don't want to make this more difficult than it has to be with avoidance. We've got to face this thing. In the meantime, we have to keep looking for a way to resolve it," Doran said.

"You know how to fix mom back dad?" Ina asked with a glimmer of excitement.

"Let's not say "fix" your mom Ina. We don't want to make it seem like something is wrong with her. But yes, I do want us to learn more about this and see if it's happened to someone else and see how they resolved it, *if* they resolved it," Doran explained.

"Oh ok. Well I hope we can figure that out soon dad," Ina agreed.

"I don't even know where to begin looking for answers. First of all if we asked around no one would ever believe us. Secondly, if this happened to someone else who's to say that they ever told anyone about it. I just think we're wishing on a star here. I think I'm stuck with this body and if I'm wrong, where the hell is my body? How do I find it? Who has it? Will they be so eager to give it back? Why did they take it in the first place? Maybe it's an alien invasion!" I rambled.

"Baby ---" Doran began before he was interrupted by the waitress who was bringing our food to the table.

"Ummmm yours looks good dad," Ina said.

"You want to try some?" Doran asked reaching for a spoon.

"Yeah I wanna try some," Ina answered.

Doran gave her a spoonful once the waitress put her plate down.

We were all quiet as we got situated to eat.

Reaching over onto Doran's plate and getting some of his food with her spoon and seemingly a bit hesitant, Ina said, "Ummm I like it dad!" taking in a bite-sized serving of his dish.

"Yeah it's pretty good. How is yours baby?" Doran said looking over at me as I swallowed the second bite.

"It's delish! I'll definitely have to order it again. It's good to try new things. hanh?" I said looking at Ina.

We were all quiet for a while as we enjoyed our food. Apparently we were all pretty hungry because we all damn near licked our plates clean. We finished up, Doran paid the tab and we headed back to the car.

"So where to next ladies?" Doran said with an adventurous grin.

8

I wasn't really in the mood to push this *adventure* any further, but I knew that Doran was right and that I couldn't stay holed up in the house forever. In fact, I would have to face that reality as early as the next day since I had to teach classes at the studio. So I tried to think of where we should head to next.

Before I could say anything Ina blurted out, "Let's go to the mall dad!"

I cringed at the thought. There was no way I was going to a mall. That was just too much too soon and I was no way near being ready for all of that. There would undoubtedly be tons of people there. More than that we'd get more stares than enough and I didn't want to face that yet.

"No way. I'm no way near ready for all of that," I objected.

"Now baby it's actually a good idea. What better way to dive into this thing. If you can survive a trip to the mall than you can survive anything. You are a survivor baby. You always have been and I know you can get control of this situation. Come on. Let's do it. We're both here with you and you know we have your back. I don't care what other peoples stares say. We know who you are and you know who you are. To be honest I think you're looking at this thing all wrong. If I was a white man for a day I would be the first one going out and taking advantage of all the perks that come along with that," Doran said.

"What? I'm living through a nightmare right now and you're talking about perks," I snapped.

"Yes perks! That's the problem baby. This doesn't have to be a nightmare. Just think of all the opportunities your white skin will afford you. In fact, let's test it out at the mall. Come on. Let's try it out. You might just like it. If I had white skin I'd do something like go apply for a business loan, buy a house, ask for a raise, join a country club and all the other things white skin affords you. I'm telling you that you're looking at this thing all wrong baby," Doran said laughing.

I thought about it and Doran did have a point. "Babe you are crazy," I laughed with him.

Totally oblivious to what we were talking about Ina interrupted and asked, "So are we going to the mall mom?"

"I guess so," I said hesitantly.

"Yaaayyyy!" Ina cheered.

"Alright! To the mall it is," Doran said.

I knew that he would probably go to Pentagon City Mall, which was about 15 minutes away in Northern Virginia and just as I expected that's just where Doran went. The mall wasn't too crowded, but crowded enough. When we first got there I felt like all eyes were on me. I started to feel so anxious. I started to perspire. My heart seemed to pound out of my chest and my white washed face was flush.

Doran looked at me with a look of concern and said, "Baby you have to calm yourself down."

"I know and I'm trying," I said trying to control my breathing as I spoke.

My throat was so dry that I could barely swallow. I took in a deep breath and tried to calm myself down as best I could. It wasn't working. I just started to feel like the walls were caving in on me.

I looked around and it was like all eyes were on me. Then everything went black. I don't remember what happened after that. I just remember seeing Ina and Doran sitting on both sides of me on a mall bench.

"Baby are you okay?" Doran asked with a look of worry.

"What happened?" I asked.

"You passed out! Luckily when you did we were close enough to this bench where we sat you down so as not to draw any attention to you. What happened baby? Are you okay?" Doran asked still very concerned.

"Yeah mom. You scared me to death!" Ina said almost panicking.

"I'm sorry Ina. I'm okay. I just think I got a little overly anxious. I just need a second to get myself together. I'm okay though," I said reassuringly.

I could tell that neither of them were convinced. I sat still for another couple of minutes trying to calm my breathing and slow down my heart rate. Soon I was relaxed. Doran, who was holding my hand the whole time could feel the tension in my hands gradually relax.

"So are you ready to try this again baby?" he asked looking into my eyes.

"Yeah I'm ready now. Let's do this," I answered.

We all got up and started walking through the mall. This time I avoided everyone's eyes. I walked through the mall as if I were in my own skin. I decided to heed Doran's advice and change my attitude about the whole thing.

Seeing the change in my demeanor and apparently sensing the change in my energy Doran looked over at me and smiled. I knew why he was smiling so I smiled back.

"So you're getting the hang of this thing I see," Doran said.

"A little. I'm just coming into some level of acceptance of it. I'm realizing that my resistance of it isn't doing me any good. So I'm just approaching it a different way," I said.

"Well that's a good start baby. I'm proud of you for that," Doran said.

"Yeah so let's do this babe. I'm ready," I said with my head held high walking forward.

In that instant I was in a different space. I was deep in the unknown, deeper than I'd ever been. I had no idea where I was headed in my new skin. I had no idea about the why of it all. I just knew that I had to be the one to bring myself into the knowing of it all. This happened to me and me alone and it happened to me for a reason. I had to get to the root of of it and that meant that I had to lose the fear and figure things out.

Just as I was deep in thought about it all the most bizarre thing happened. I looked up and what I saw shook me to the core! My face turned flush. My heart began beating out of my chest, I got shortness of breath and my entire reality took a drastic turn. Still holding my hand and seeing and feeling the change in my energy Doran turned toward me and looked at my face then followed my eyes to see what I saw. It shocked us both the very core.

Oblivious to what was happening Ina grabbed my other hand and said, "Ooooh mom can we see a movie?" pointing to the movie theatre just ahead of us.

9

Before Doran could stop me I broke my hands free from he and Ina. I headed towards a woman who was just a few feet away. This was no random woman. In fact, she looked just like me, the REAL me! So in what seemed like less than an instant I broke free of Doran and Ina and ran toward the woman guns a blazing. It was totally out of character for me to respond so aggressively, but nothing about this situation was normal.

The woman hadn't spotted me yet so I expected that when I came up to her she would have been caught completely off guard. However, it was just the opposite. She slowly and calmly turned around and smiled at me as if she was expecting me. Having been prepared to go at her with all 10 claws I was the one caught off guard by her response. Before I could say anything Doran had come over looking just as shocked as I was.

"Who are you?" Doran blurted out to the woman who was alone and casually walking through the mall.

"I'm your wife. Can't you see that?" the woman said matter-of-factly.

"No you're not!" I yelled getting even more agitated.

"The true question is who are *you*? Do you even know?" the woman asked staring at me blankly.

I had no come back because at that moment I truly *didn't* know who I was. I thought I did before then, but since I'd woken up that morning as someone else all of that changed. I was living the life of someone I was clueless about. Over night it seemed that all that I thought I knew of who I was went out the window and the next thing I knew I was a stranger to even myself. The woman was absolutely right. I *didn't* know who I was.

However, I also didn't know who she was and that was something that I had to find out. So I asked her, "So who are you?"

"I am you, the you that you don't yet know. Though, when you are ready you *will* know me," the woman said as she turned to walk away.

"Where are you going? You have to tell me what's going on here? Why and how did this even happen? Will I change back? Am I stuck in this body forever?" I asked anxiously.

"The answers to all of *those* questions will come. In the meantime you should know that you aren't quite focusing on the right questions at the moment. Focus inward a bit more and more will be revealed to you. Know that you're right where you need to be. There are no mistakes. Always remember that," the woman said.

Before I could say anything else she was gone and Doran and I were left standing there frozen. We each had a thousand questions buzzing through our minds.

"What the hell just happened?" I said perplexed as ever.

"Things have gotten even stranger now," Doran responded.

"Yeah," I said staring blankly into space.

I was a thousand miles away, deep in thought about what the woman who appeared to be me had said. I wondered what she meant when she said that I wasn't quite focusing on the right questions. What questions were the *right* questions? More importantly, what did she mean when she said that there were no mistakes. If this *wasn't* a mistake it certainly *was* a nightmare. Replaying it all over again in my head was making me get anxious again and in the white skin it was all too obvious so I tried to calm myself down before my skin turned flush.

"Babe can we get out of here?" I asked.

"Yeah I think that would be best. Ina I'll take you to see whatever movie you want to see another time, but for now we have to head back home," Doran said gesturing for us to head back to our car.

"Ok dad. I understand. Who was that lady that you two were talking to? She looked just like mom," Ina inquired.

"We don't know," I answered.

"Yeah, but we're gonna find out," Doran added making eye contact with me as we walked hurriedly back to the mall entrance.

We walked back to the car then rode the entire way home in silence each very immersed in our own thoughts. When I got back to the house I decided that I needed to spend some alone time in the meditation room. Since that day I hadn't really gotten a chance to be alone to try to process the whole thing I desperately needed that time.

During stressful times our meditation room was like a mini nirvana. Not only was it conservatively decorated with an alter, pictures and statues of various deities and ancestors and a very impressive collection of crystals, it also provided access to the roof. I called it our rooftop escape and it was where we sometimes enjoyed rooftop barbeques and where I had created the most beautiful zen garden. It was like our little year round escape from the world. Both Doran and I meditated often so the room got lots of use. Besides that we both did our perspective forms of martial arts there since we both preferred practicing our arts alone. While I did yoga Doran had practiced Kung Fu and Tai Chi for years before I met him so he used the room for that.

From the moment I stepped into the front door I knew that the meditation room was exactly what I needed. I needed to do some yoga to calm my nerves and so I did. I changed into some black leggings and a black tank top then headed into the meditation room. I rolled out my yoga mat then began by taking in a deep inhale as I raised my arms outstretched toward the sky into mountain pose.

Then I began doing a series of sun salutation sequences to loosen up and release some of the tension out of my muscles. The more I repeated the sequence the better I began to feel. I started to feel like me again.   For a moment I forgot about being in someone else's body. I remembered how it felt to be in the world of wonder and questions and for a moment I felt good again.

10

It had been 4 days since the body swap. We'd come up with a cover story that I was away training to get a master yoga instructor certificate and that a substitute instructor who was a distant cousin by marriage was running the studio in my absence. Doran stepped up a lot more to help transport Ina to and from school, activities and social outings. It seemed that we had come up with a pretty good work around for our issue.

I still had not gotten used to my imposter body and had to fight like hell to resist the urge to look at it every time I passed a mirror. I didn't want to see her because seeing her made the whole thing seem too real and too permanent. The last thing I wanted was for it to be permanent.

The most difficult thing for me to adjust to was my new hair. It was a lot more stringy and smelly than I was used to, especially if I didn't wash it everyday. Besides that I had to go out and buy all new hair products just to manage it.

I also had a hard time getting used to my skin. It was just so pale and lifeless. I felt like everything about me was lifeless from my hair and my skin to how I felt inside. It was an adjustment that I just felt I'd never be able to make.

Like me, Doran was making what I considered very fruitless efforts to hide his feelings toward her. Nonetheless, I could feel the difference in his touch. Besides that he didn't want to make love. He was usually the initiator and since the swap he hadn't made the slightest move on her.

I wasn't hurt by it though because as weird as it was I felt that he was being loyal to my true self and I loved him for that. Part of me felt like if he shared intimacy with her he may as well have cheated on me and that would have been unforgivable. So I felt no less loved by him despite his lack of intimacy over the past few days.

Being in the imposter body also had it's impact on Ina as well. She wasn't her usual clingy, super affectionate, huggable, loveable self with her. Yet again, I understood and was in no way offended by it.

We were all dealing with her the best way that we could. Meanwhile, I was still searching for answers and solutions as was Doran.

The most drastic and difficult change that we faced was that I really didn't go out much. I pretty much went to the studio, the grocery store and returned home. Doran and I weren't the social butterflies that we usually were going to all the community events together. In fact, there was a workshop coming up that we were already registered for that we had to make a decision about. About a month earlier we had registered for the

Divine Marriage Workshop and it was scheduled to be held on the upcoming weekend.

I really didn't know what I was going to do. I felt that neither Doran nor I was ready for such an outing. We both knew that there probably wouldn't be any white people there and that I would stand out like a sore thumb, which was an issue that we'd soon have to address. I knew that I wasn't ready to address it and I was pretty sure that Doran wasn't either.

Then, as if reading my mind and only moments into my thoughts Doran asked, "So baby are we going to the workshop this weekend?"

"I was just wondering the same thing. I don't know that we're ready for an outing like that, but at the same time I know we *need* to go, especially now with what's going on," I replied.

"You're right about that. We do *need* to go. The only concern that I have is how we will each deal with the response from others. I already know that me walking in there with a white girl will bring about a lot of stares," Doran responded.

"Yes, those are my thoughts as well. I don't know babe, I just don't know," I added.

"Well there's two choices. We can keep hiding in here or we can keep living our lives. We've been looking forward to this workshop for weeks. I know that we'll gain a wealth of knowledge by going whereas staying here will only result in us being in the same place headed nowhere. That said, I think we should go. We'll deal with the stares when we get there," Doran said.

"Wow. Well I guess that says it all. I'm with you babe. If you say we should go then I think we should too. Let's do it!" I agreed.

Even with that matter resolved I was still feeling anxious about it. However, after what Doran had said I at least felt a lot more prepared to face my fears. Besides that I knew that Doran would have my back so I tried not to worry too much about it.

It was getting late so I decided to get dinner started. I had a craving for breakfast food so I made breakfast food for dinner. I pulled out all of the stops. I made homemade waffles with fresh strawberries and veggie sausages.

"Dinner is ready!" I yelled to Ina and Doran.

"Ummmm mom smells like breakfast for dinner, my favorite!" Ina said nearly sprinting into the kitchen.

We had an eat-in kitchen with a mid-sized glass round table that seated 4. I set the waffles, sliced strawberries and sausages in the center of the table along with some freshly squeezed orange and mango juice that I made in the juicer.

"Wow this feels like the old you is back baby. This looks good. I miss meals like this," Doran said smiling.

"Yeah so do I. That's why I prepared it. We haven't done this in a long time, at least not since the change. It seems like I've been this way forever. I figured waiting for me to change back is stopping me from living now so this is my first step in that direction. I still gotta live," I said.

"I agree. You do have to live and I'm happy to see you beginning to do that again," Doran said as he reached in with his fork to get a waffle.

"I'm not saying that I've got this thing worked out, but I definitely know that even while I'm mentally coming to grips with this thing I also have to keep living," I added.

"Well baby we understand. We may not be going through what you're going through, but we're here with you while you do. I still don't know how or why this happened and perhaps we never will. I've been researching this thing to death and have still come up empty. It seems this really *is* one of those freak things that just happened. Have you come across anything yet? Able to make any sense of what that lady in the mall said? Gotten any signs or symbols on what may be going on in your meditations?" Doran inquired.

"Actually I have. Just yesterday during my meditation I got a strong feeling of being two people. It was like both of them were extremes and they were at war trying to find their balance. The feeling was so strong that I almost felt like I was being pulled into opposite directions. One was so warm and loving while the other gave me a sensation of heaviness. It was like a Jehkyl and Hyde sensation," I explained.

"Hmmm that actually makes a lot of sense in light of what's going on. In a lot of ways you *are* being pulled in two directions. You're struggling to maintain your sense of self while also trying to embrace the new set of circumstances you've been dealt in light of this change," Doran suggested.

Ina was chomping away at the pile of strawberries that she'd piled on top of her waffles while Doran and I talked so she was oblivious to what we were even discussing.

"I still often look in the mirror though and ask myself, who ARE you? Cause in a sense I feel like I have no idea. I feel like what I thought I knew of me I no longer feel so confident in knowing. It feels like I'm a stranger to myself," I explained.

"Well trust me we all feel that way. I always get the feeling like this is all a dream. It's like a dream you just can't wake yourself up from. Do you feel that way too?" Doran asked.

"I sure do babe. It's weird. I always felt that, but I feel it even more now. I don't know maybe we *are* all in a dream," I said trailing off deep into my own thoughts as I continued eating.

"Maybe this is the beginning of our waking up. I think the mere fact that we're consciously thinking that we are dreaming even suggests that," Doran added seemingly going deeper into his own thoughts as well.

Doran was always a deep brothah. It's what drew me to him. I always loved that he wasn't one to take on anyone else's truth but his own. He had his own ideologies, not what he read in a book or was conditioned to believe through associations with any groups, religions or family members. He was his own guru and I found that so sexy! This was important to me because I was always a think and live outside-of-the-box kind of girl who a lot of people couldn't relate to. I always danced to the beat of my own drum and never subscribed to anyone's belief system.

So Doran was perfect for me. He was the most open-minded person that I knew. He never judged, down-played, belittled or disrespected anyone else's beliefs. He never looked to prove himself to anyone and never needed to have followers. In fact, he spent most of his free time alone studying and doing his own inner work discovering his own truth. He was definitely his own man. I would sometimes just sit and gaze at him in awe. Then, just like on the day that we met, in that moment I saw him for who he was, a God.

Just as that thought crossed my mind I thought to myself, "So what does that make me?"

11

The weekend had arrived and it was time for Doran and I to head to the Divine Marriage workshop. Ina was at a friends for a sleepover playdate. Doran had dropped her off while I got dressed and tried to get my nerves ready for the workshop.

I just didn't know how the community would receive Doran and I as a couple with me as my white self. It was usually frowned upon for a brothah to come to such an event with a white chick. So I couldn't believe that *I* was "the white chick" at the event! I still wondered why on earth this was happening to me? Couldn't it have happened to someone else?

I tried to get my mind off of what I wasn't able to control at the moment and focused instead on the workshop. I'd been looking forward to it for weeks and I just couldn't bring myself to miss it even in the face of such a devastating personal situation. Something was telling me that I needed to be there no matter what and so I kept getting dressed.

I rummaged through my closet for what felt like hours trying to decide what to wear. Given that I was in my white skin I didn't want to go looking too ethnic because I didn't want to look like one of those corny ass white girls trying too hard to look 'down.' At the same time I didn't want to look too mainstream because I didn't want to look like the white girl who just didn't quite belong.

Eventually I decided on just wearing jeans and a brown t-shirt. I figured it was as neutral as I could go. I put my hair up in the usual bun and wore some light brown lip gloss. I hadn't worn make-up of any kind in what seemed like forever since I'd been in my white body so it felt kind of good to put a little gloss on.

"Wow you almost look like your old self, only a little more pale," Doran joked as he came into the room looking at me.

"Come on babe. I'm trying and this is hard for me," I sulked.

"You look fine. I think you've made a good choice taking the neutral route," Doran replied as if instinctively knowing my outfit selection process.

"Thanks for noticing that because that's exactly what I was doing," I answered.

"So are you about ready? We have to get a move on so we can get a good seat," Doran asked hurriedly.

"Yeah... I'm as ready as I'm gonna get. What about you? Are you ready to face this crowd?" I inquired.

"I sure am. We have a great cover story to quell the questions. Since we're saying you're family no one will suspect an affair or betrayal to the sistahs so to speak," Doran answered laughing.

"Yeah I guess you're right. It should be fine. I keep forgetting about the cover story. In that case it will be fine. I'm ready. Let's go," I said grabbing my purse and jacket.

We both headed for the workshop and though I knew that all would be well I was still nervous as hell the entire ride there. I kept playing the whole thing out in my head of how I thought things might play out. It would either be a disaster or perfectly fine. I chose to go with the latter and began to calm myself down as we arrived and Doran parked the car. I looked at the building that seemed way too close.

"Ready or not here we go baby!" Doran shouted as he turned the car off.

"I know. I guess I'm ready. Let's just do it. The longer I sit in here the more I'll try to talk myself out of it. So let's just go," I said reaching for the door handle to open my own door.

Doran ran around to meet me on my side and grabbed my door. I hopped out as confidently as I could under the circumstances. Though inside it felt like my heart was about to pound out of my chest and my stomach was on a washing machine spin cycle. My mind was racing. I had shortness of breath and my mouth became as dry as the Sahara desert. I looked up at the building and there seemed to be a million steps between us. Each step that I took toward it seemed like a step closer to my death sentence.

I thought to myself, "This is worse than death. What am I doing here? Am I crazy?" Again as if reading my thoughts Doran gave me a reassuring look as we approached the front door of the building and he walked ahead of me to open it.

He whispered in my ear, "Just breathe baby. Just breathe."

I nodded feeling a slight sense of relief in knowing that I was not going through this alone. I still carried the weight of my own thoughts as I walked the walk of shame trailing behind Doran as we approached the check-in table. For some reason I didn't feel worthy of walking beside him. Doran was a strong, fine as hell black man who all black women with working eyes adored. Despite what we were going through he still handled himself with such confidence. He was so in control and exuded such self-assurance.

Meanwhile, I felt like the scum of the earth in my white skin. I felt ashamed as if I had in someway wronged someone. I felt afraid. I felt the stares of everyone around pierce me like a sword. Again my breathing became more shallow. I thought that at any moment I would just faint, but I talked myself out of that because I didn't want to bring anymore attention to myself than was already on me.

Then it seemed that instantly we were at our seats. I was so lost in the hell of my own thoughts that I couldn't even remember how we got there. The venue wasn't the fanciest. In fact, it was kind of a hole in the wall. It was an old house that seemed to have been transformed into a meeting hall. The walls needed a fresh coat of paint, the floors weren't leveled and the windows were old and drafty. It was located in the heart of the city in N.W., D.C. not far from Howard University on Irving St.

In somewhat of a haze I sat down quickly and lowered my head down almost curling up in the seat as if it was a safety net. I looked around slowly taking detailed notes of my surroundings. I took mental notes of who was sitting near me, whether or not they seemed bothered by my presence. I looked at how visible I was to the speaker and tried to determine whether I would be a distraction. I looked at how close to the end of the row I was in case I needed to make a quick exit. I also looked around to see if there were any other interracial couples there. It was then that I got the shock of my life!

12

To my surprise, as I glanced around the room I noticed that there were in fact *several* other interracial couples in attendance. I had to close my eyes for a few seconds then re-open them again to take a second look to make sure that I wasn't seeing things. I thought for sure that my eyes were playing tricks on me.

I looked to the front of us and there was a sistah that I remembered seeing at some other events sitting there with this average height, slim white dude with dark hair that sort of favored Taylor Lautner from the Twilight saga. In fact, for a split second I thought that for a white guy he was kinda hot!

Then I looked to the left of us and saw a brothah with a white, dark-haired girl who resembled Keira Knightley. Next, to the right of us I could have sworn the white girl that another brothah was with was Alyssa Milano! Everywhere I looked I saw an interracial couple. It was like some sort of epidemic.

Then just as quickly as that thought came to mind Doran turned to me and blurted out, "Wow, either white is the new black or there is some type of epidemic going on. Are you seeing what I'm seeing?"

"Yes and I was just thinking the same thing! What the hell is going on? This can't be a coincidence. I think that what happened to me has happened to a lot of other people here babe. This is so weird. I wonder what this means?" I replied.

Just as Doran and I were discussing the "epidemic" a couple seated in front of us turned around as if overhearing our conversation and joined in. "It's definitely an epidemic and weird doesn't begin to describe it," a medium-sized white guy sitting with a chocolate, natural-haired sistah blurted out.

Doran and I looked at him then looked at each other both wondering whether it was okay to share with him what happened to me. Before we could he started telling us his story.

"A few days ago our entire life changed," he said grabbing ahold of the sistah's hand. "I went to sleep as a brothah and woke up like this. I have no explanation as to how or why it happened. Nor do I know how to reverse it. Since then my wife and I have been trying to find out more information. We weren't gonna come here tonight, but figured we should since we had tickets and since we typically don't miss these events. Now that we're here I see that we're not alone. I wonder if they will discuss it at all in the workshop. I know it wasn't the planned topic, but it sure as hell needs to be addressed. It seems to be spreading across the black community like wildfire. Anyway enough about me, what's you guys story?"

I looked at his wife and she looked at me intensely with inquiring eyes. I looked at Doran as I was a bit nervous about disclosing so he answered. Besides that I wasn't sure if we were still going with the cover story or not.

"Same story man. We have no idea what's going on. It's definitely not the type of thing that you go around asking about so we've been laying low and doing the research quietly trying to figure things out on our own. Good to know we're not alone at least. From the looks of things it'll definitely be the topic of discussion tonight," Doran said looking around the room.

"Yeah you got that right. I can't wait to hear what others have to say about the situation. I really wanna know if there is a way to reverse it. Not that being a white guy hasn't come with its perks cause man I been introduced to a whole new reality in this skinsuit!" the guy said jokingly.

We all laughed along. "But seriously I need my own body back. All the same I'm doing all I can to change our life for the better while I have this one," he said laughing. We all laughed together.

Just then a tall, light-skinned brothah with a goatee walked up to the microphone, "Peace everyone. So glad to see that you all made it out once again. As most of you know I'm brothah Kwan and this is our 3rd year doing the Divine Marriage workshop. Glad you all could make it. We have a lot of good information for ya'll tonight, especially with regards to the obvious questions that ya'll probably have about what the hell is going on," he said looking around the room with raised eyebrows.

"In fact, before we get started I want to go ahead and address it. I've heard from a lot of you that some real strange things have been going on in the community. I know first hand what ya'll are talking about because the same thing happened to me, well maybe not to me, but to my wife, Alicia," he began then took a long pause.

We all sat on the edge of our seats waiting for him to say the words. We were all thinking it and more than that we were living this nightmare and couldn't wait for the opportunity to openly discuss it. So we all stared at Kwan intensely waiting for him to blurt it out. It seemed that once he did we could all exhale.

We had all been so nervous and uptight while struggling with trying to deal with the circumstances of our changed bodies. It was a welcomed surprise to be in a room full of others who too were living out the same nightmare and so when Kwan brought it up we all felt a huge weight lifted. We couldn't wait to hear him say the words out loud. It seemed that hearing the words publicly out loud made it easier to accept. More than that hearing that others out there were going through it made it easier to cope.

Kwan looked around the room then continued, "A few days ago I woke up to find that my beautiful, brown-skinned wife Alicia had transformed into a white woman. At first, I thought that it was some sick joke and that Alicia was somewhere hiding. Then after coming to grips with the fact that the white woman *was* Alicia I faced the most difficult 3 days of my life. It was a lot harder for Alicia than it was for me. She has barely been able to sleep. She won't come out of the room and I've been lying to my kids about what's going on with her. We've been living a nightmare. I'm looking around the room right now and from the looks on your faces I see that I'm not alone. When it first happened I didn't know what to do. I was afraid to tell anyone because I thought for sure they'd think I was crazy. But then my man Ron came by scared as hell saying that something happened to his queen. I knew what he meant before he finished the sentence. After that I heard one story after the next, each describing the same thing."

Kwan paused and took a long look at all of us. He then continued taking on an even more serious tone. "Something is happening to us and it's big. It's not happening to all of us, but it is happening to those certain ones of us on what I'll say is on a certain frequency. In other words, some of us have tuned into a certain radio station and picked up on certain radio waves if you know what I mean. What that means is that if you're here, you are obviously one of those few. More than that, if you know what I'm talking about you definitely are one of the few. I know that like me you have a lot of questions about what is going on and I don't really have any answers. However, what I *do* know is that this all has something to do with the Divine Marriage. What I've learned is that everyone of us who came, planned on coming and thought about coming to this workshop has been affected by this.... 'phenomenon.' Yes everyone of us," Kwan continued over the whispers that had begun to penetrate what was moments prior a dead silent room.

"I know that might have ya'll buggin even more, but that's what I've learned so far. What I also know is that this workshop is a very special workshop. We have some very powerful information to share with you all tonight as we said in all of the advertisements. This year's workshop isn't going to be like the others. This workshop is going to take us all to the next level. Now I don't know if that has anything to do with what's going on or not, but I do know that it can't just be a coincidence. Anyway, I know that I haven't answered any of your questions, but I hope that I have at least eased your minds a bit. What I propose that we do to get more answers is to proceed with tonight's workshop as planned. I have a strong feeling that as we go through the workshop the answers will come. In fact, I feel that something huge is going to transpire here tonight. So I want you all to just be open to receive tonight's share," Kwan concluded.

We all nodded in agreement, though with the look of a million more questions floating around in our heads. Nonetheless, we settled ourselves as we prepared to focus on the workshop and let things flow as they may.

I grabbed ahold of Doran's hand, then unafraid of what others thought of our interracial pairing as I was comforted by his company. He looked over at me and smiled grabbing my hand tighter.

I didn't know what to expect and part of me didn't expect anything. Though at the same time I was very certain that I was ready for everything. It was weird, but with all that had already transpired it was the first time in days that I felt any sense of certainty about anything even as weird as this certainty was.

13

We all got settled in our seats and looked straight ahead at Kwan as if all in agreement and preparing to take the journey forward together. I felt like I was on the Starship Enterprise or something preparing to explore new life, new civilizations and boldly go where no man has gone before. I felt like Scotty had just beamed me up.

Just then Kwan introduced the guest speaker who was someone we'd never heard speak at any of the other events, but who we were all very familiar with as she was a popular author of a book entitled, "The Black Universe." Her name was Connie Murphy and she was what many of us considered a literary oracle. Her books were fiction, but to us that was a mere technical term.

We all firmly believed that Connie was a master channeler, meaning she received and communicated messages from the spiritual realm. She was a deep sistah very in tuned with her spirituality. It was Doran who had introduced me to her books. Prior to reading them I was probably not what most would have considered the most spiritual person or anyone who was too into the woo woo stuff. However, Doran changed all of that by introducing me to Connie's books.

Connie did her research too and was quite knowledgeable about what many considered the metaphysical. After reading her books my whole perspective on the subject had forever changed. So I was pleasantly surprised that she was the guest speaker. From the looks on everyone else's face so were they.

Connie was a short, stocky sistah with long, well-maintained locs. For as short as she was she had a very commanding presence. She had the most piercing eyes and when she looked at you it seemed that she saw clear through to your soul.

Connie began organizing her papers as Kwan pointed to a pitcher of water and a glass that had been prepared for her before she moved toward the microphone. There was no stage in the room so they used a podium with a microphone attached that had a small area where the speaker could rest any papers with notes. There was also a small table located behind the podium where Connie had stored more materials. She also had a clicker for a slide show presentation that was paused and ready to be projected onto the wall behind her.

We all sat alert and eager for Connie to begin. She looked up, smiled warmly then greeted us, "Peace everyone!"

We all replied, "Peace."

"I see ya'll ready for me to tell you something good this evening, but looking around I have a question for you! Man so what the hell is going on? Yes, I'm asking the same question as you! I promise you this whole thing has got me trippin too. I've never seen nothing like it. Now what I *will* say is that this is happening to us all over the place. It's not just happening here. I've been on the road on a book tour for the past few months and I've seen it happening everywhere. I guess that's why they asked me to speak to ya'll. I heard that it just happened here over the past week or so. But let me tell you it's been happening other places longer than that. I know ya'll want to know what *it* is and I hate to tell you but I don't have any definitive answers. I *can* tell you something about it based on my work and what I've decoded thus far, but you each still have to do your own work to figure out for yourselves what it means for you," Connie began to explain.

The instant Connie began asking about the strange things that were going on the energy in the entire room shifted as everyone seemed to be on the edge of their seats eager to hear her thoughts on the matter.

I think I even stopped breathing for what seemed like 10 minutes. I couldn't believe how much had changed for me in so short a period of time. For starters, I had no idea when I woke up this morning that the day would unfold as it had. Since leaving home everything as I knew it had changed. Then, over the past few days my life had been turned upside down and it was getting crazier by the minute. What I'd seen and heard over the past several minutes blew my mind and it seemed that there was no way that any of it could be real. However, I knew that it was real because I was living it. So I knew that as sure as I was breathing air it was real.

Though lately, I began to question what was real anyway? I wondered if what I thought to be real all along was truly real. Who was to say that what we thought was real truly was. It could have been just that we were taught and conditioned to believe it to be so.

I sat there waiting for Connie to continue with a million questions like that buzzing through my mind a mile a minute. I didn't know what to believe anymore. I didn't even know whether I believed my own eyes anymore. For all I know I was dreaming all of this up and had been for some time. Perhaps I was beginning to wake up and I really was white.

Then I began to wonder if maybe I'd been transported to some other time period or some other place. Maybe life as I knew it really wasn't. Who was I anyway? I'd always felt so out of place anyway. It seemed the only one who got me was Doran, which was why we were so quickly drawn to one another. It seemed one day we met and the next we were married almost like it was all one action. Doran could always answer all of my questions no matter how quirky. He never judged me for questioning nor did he poke fun at me. In fact, he seemed to share in my inquisitiveness. It was a trait that we both had in common among other things.

As my mind buzzed with a million thoughts Doran looked over at me as if reading my mind as usual.

He knew what I was thinking and was likely wondering the same things. Moments seemed like an eternity as we waited for Connie to continue. She took a long pause before continuing and appeared to be channelling. She had closed her eyes for a few moments then looked out at us with a dazed look almost as if she was looking past us. However, the intensity in her stare let us know that all of her attention was directed toward us.

As Connie parted her lips to speak I inhaled deeply finally taking a breath and feeling an eerie sense of calm overcome me. My heart rate slowed, my shoulders relaxed and my jaws loosened and I was open and ready to receive her message. It was time for the revelation of what I'd been living through over the past few days and everything in me knew it. I was ready. In fact, we all were and it could be felt throughout the room as the energy had shifted once again.

14

The room was quiet enough to hear a pin drop as we all sat on the edge of our seats anticipating what felt like a long awaited revelation. It was clearly written on everyone's face that we all just wanted to regain some control over what was happening to us. We all felt like something else had taken control over our very reality and it was an unwelcomed feeling.

After what seemed like an eternity Connie parted her lips and uttered the first word of power, at least that's what it felt like. It seemed that anyone with some form of an explanation had the power, not so much over us personally as over our collective destiny. We all wanted our power back and knowing gave us a sense of regaining just that.

"Before I begin I want you all to know that what I'm about to tell you is what I received through a channel. That said, nothing that I say is written in stone. In fact, you each may come into an entirely different explanation so don't take it as your sole truth," Connie explained before pausing.

"As I was writing, doing some work on my most recent book I was overcome by a strong urge to go to a mirror. So I followed the urge and when I got to the mirror I couldn't believe my eyes. Like many of you I saw a white woman staring back at me. She appeared to be a white version of me. Now for me this wasn't surprising, nor did it scare me as many of my channels occur in this way. In fact, it was something that I always had a curiosity about."

Then briefly pausing she continued, "So anyway, I calmly looked at her in the mirror and began to speak to her. I started by asking her what she wanted me to know. She replied by saying that she was me from a past life and that she had appeared to me in this life because the energy from that lifetime had come back online. She went on to explain that I existed in her form during a time when we were all colorless. It was a time when we were in a lower form plagued by a lot of fear and hatred. That was our normal state of being at that time and we knew of nothing else as we had succumb to a highly intense emotional state. During that time emotion ruled over us. We had lost all sense of spirituality over the course of our descent into this form and were a warring world. All we did was fight. We existed in a perpetual state of resistance and savagery. She explained to me that this wasn't our original form, but it was a form that we had taken on as a result of succumbing to our emotions. So it was a part of our history in which we descended, a part that we had somehow blocked out," Connie explained.

We all began to get more uneasy as we listened on. No doubt others throughout the room were questioning what Connie was saying. We had never before heard of anything like it and many of us were simply not prepared to receive it. It appeared to be a dark period of our past that had seemingly come back to haunt us like the ghost that many of us saw in the mirror staring back at us.

I certainly had questions about Connie's share. If what she said was true, why was this happening to certain ones of us. Were we more hateful than others? Were we being punished for past behaviors? Was this going to happen to all of us? What could we do to reverse it? Was there even a way to reverse it? These and many other questions ran through my mind as I listened on.

"I know that this wasn't what you were probably expecting to hear, but its what I got. Now I don't know if this means that we're heading for descent rather than ascent, but if nothing else we can take it as a warning. It may be a warning of what is to come if we don't quickly make some changes. Perhaps we are not doing enough to ascend. Perhaps we are not focused enough. Perhaps we are too easily influenced by the distractions of this time. Perhaps we are not loving enough. Perhaps we have strayed too far from who we truly are. Whatever the case its a sign that we have work to do and we need to do it quickly. I've been on tour traveling the world for the past several months and this thing seems to be spreading like the plague. I wouldn't be surprised if soon the entire world isn't white-washed. What's more is that soon, not only will you all *look* white, but you will begin to *act* like them and take on their less than desirable, annoying characteristics," Connie continued looking around the room.

"You each know what I'm talking about," she said pausing momentarily. "The arrogance, selfishness, childishness and superiority complex that we've all had to live with. So be very mindful of your emotions. The full descent into this form could sneak up on you like a thief in the night. It's an energy that is predatory in nature so do not fall prey to it. It fact, it is our ignorance of our rightful place as predators that has gotten us into this bind."

We all looked around the room at each other confused as ever by what Connie had just said. What did she mean, we were predators? We had a history of being a peaceful people. We never preyed on the weak. If anything that behavior had always been linked to our white counterpart. The more I listened on the more I began to question what Connie was saying.

"Looking at your faces I know that what I just said has shocked you. I know that it's not something that you're used to hearing and you're probably not even ready to accept it, but it's true. It's your truth. It's a truth that's been hidden from you and that you've been programmed to forget. You've been programmed to be cattle, sheep…. prey. Think about it, in your religions you're told to *pray* and are then herded around like cattle while waiting for something outside of yourself to solve your problems and save you. You're told that maintaining the herd mentality is the preferred manner of thinking. You're told to follow the Word of God, the laws of man, the rules of your parents and school. If you do anything to the contrary you're punished and ostracized. Meanwhile, those telling you to do these things do not do as you do. Without you as their flock they would be nothing, they could not feed, they could not survive as the parasites they are. Yet.... there are those among us who've been misguided into being prey, who aren't meant to be prey, whose divine purpose is to be among the predators who've come here tasked with a divine mission to prevent our descent further into this lower form. We know who we are. It's each of us sitting in this room right now. If you weren't one among the predators you would not be here right now. You would not hear the message that I'm delivering to you. The truth is that we come from a long line of predators and we have left the evidence of that all around us despite what we've been taught. Look around and you'll see. I'll give you a hint, starting with your own ancient mythology. Now that's all. The rest is up to you. This situation will continue to unfold whether you choose to research this further or not. Yet how it unfolds depends solely on you putting in the work to resolve it," Connie concluded.

With that Connie turned and stepped away from the podium. We all starred on speechless. I don't think that any of us clearly understood any of what she had said. It certainly wasn't the message that we were expecting. Then again, I'm not sure what we actually expected since everything that had already taken place was so totally unexpected.

Kwan closed out the event. Then, with looks of confusion and uncertainty we all began to file out of the building in silence and seemingly deep in thought. There was none of the usual hanging around afterwards to make small talk about the event or anything. We all just left in silence.

Enjoying this book so far? I'd love for you to share your thoughts and post a quick review on Amazon!

15

When I got into the car I immediately asked Doran, "What the hell was that?"

"Yeah I was wondering the same thing, but then I got to thinking. She's right," Doran replied.

"Hunh? Now I definitely wasn't expecting that response, but I *do* see what you're saying. Hmph.... So you believe that we are the natural predators of the world too?" I asked.

"Yeah. I do and hearing what Connie just said confirmed it. What she said awakened something in me. Like a lightbulb just came on and shed light on everything. I think it was the last thing she said when she said to look to our own ancient mythology for the answers. Think about it. She's right, our mythology tells it all. I've studied Kemetic mythology in depth and I *do* notice that all of the Neteru that are represented by animals are represented by *predatory* animals. Take for instance, Heru who is represented as a hawk and Anubis who is represented as a jackal. Then there's Tehuti who is represented as an ibis and Sekhmet who is represented as a lion. As you know there are many others, but one thing that you have to admit is that they are all represented as predatory animals," Doran continued explaining.

"Yeah but that doesn't mean we're predators. That *could* just mean that they represented the need for each of us to overcome that part of ourselves, at least that's how I see it," I rebutted.

"I agree with that also, but in a different way. I see it as our need to not allow our animal self to control our higher self. Yet still I see it as a sign that we must still maintain our status as predators rather than prey. We have to balance both lower and higher selves in the same way that the predator does. It's a unique balance which separates the predators of nature from the prey. There is something very different about predatory animals that gives them an advantage and allows them to control the kingdom and that is that they are not weakened by emotions. They kill only for their survival and for their need to feed, not for sport like their human parasitic counterparts. Their moves are focused and strategic and have a divine purpose which operates within the universal laws," Doran further explained.

As he spoke I looked at him in awe. I smiled up at him and thought to myself, "He is so damn sexy when he starts talking like this!" I loved having those intellectual conversations with Doran. It was what turned me on to him in the first place from the moment I met him. He made me so proud to call him my man.

"Then the other side of it is that for so long the black man has been told to tone down. Everything has been done to carry out that end. Yet, the very thing that is the source of our power as black men is what we've been told and conditioned to turn down. We are fearless, we are strong, we stand firm on our principals, we lead, we live according to our own truth. Meanwhile, from boys we are chastised for being this way. All the while these are the traits of a predator not prey. In fact, all things to the contrary are traits of prey. Prey live in a perpetual state of fear, are preyed upon because of their weakness, follow so they don't stand for anything and live according to the truth that they are fed," Doran continued.

"Then, "he went on, "If you're not a good boy who passively eats what he's being fed you're deemed another no-good black man, a punk or a trifling ass nigga. So the result is the black man of today who follows the rules because he is afraid of losing his job, getting arrested or killed by the cops. It's the black man of today who follows the rules because he wants to keep his family together. He follows these rules that are introduced to him as early as his toddler years that continue on into adulthood when he get's a job and these rules even make their way into his home life. Yet, these rules that he is being force-fed completely go against who he is as his own creator. Meanwhile, our women and our children, all programmed and whatnot, are worshipping the others who wouldn't dare follow these dumbass rules they're force-feeding us. And they look up to and honor these chumps as society's heroes, who have virtually duped us into trading places with them telling us to turn down so they could turn up!" Doran continued.

Coming out of the trance that he had me in I said, "Hmmm..... wow! I think you're on to something when you put it like that. I'm starting to see it now. This is some serious stuff!" I gleamed as my own lightbulb came on.

We rode the remainder of the way home in silence as I pondered all that both Connie and Doran had said. If what they were saying was true than we had all been duped. Most of the world was made up of prey and just as Connie pointed out we had all been programmed to believe that that was the way to be. We weren't encouraged to grow up and become predators. In fact, we were told that predators were the bad guys. Even more noteworthy, predators of the world had basically been wiped out, literally! There were only two types of species remaining and they were parasite and prey and the parasites were running the world while the rest of us were herded around as prey.

Delving even deeper I took a closer look and started to see that it was probably the parasites who had manipulated us into becoming prey. They camouflaged themselves as one among us and we fell for it hook, line and sinker. Ultimately, what we did was allow them to manipulate us into trading places. We were led to believe that to be the predator was to be the villain, the bad guy so to speak. Yet there was actually nothing *bad* about the predators of nature. They maintained balance in the world. They keep the prey moving forward and gave them guidance. Like Doran said they exemplified what it meant to not be controlled by your emotions. Prey only know fear as it is the primary motivation for their actions and that is what we had become as a collective.

Still going deeper into my thoughts I began to clearly see what Doran was seeing. I began to see how programmed we had all been. I began to see why our descent took place. We allowed outsiders to take control of our evolutionary path. I likened it to a mother leopard allowing a doe to teach her cub how to live as a predator in the wild. If something like that was actually to happen in nature an entire generation of leopards would become extinct. Yet, that's what happened to us. Somewhere along the way we began to die out so what was happening to us currently was a wake-up call. We had to again remember our predatory instincts and rise once again.

We had to debunk the myth that was fed to us in cartoons like *Tom & Jerry*, where Tom was the 'bad guy' and Jerry was the poor victim that needed saving. We had to debunk all the lies that we had been told since birth about who we were. It was programming at its best. The parasite had outwitted us, the predators, and it was time for us to turn the tides and once again restore balance. We had to once again see the good in Tom's role as the predatory cat whose work was to maintain balance and make sure that the world wasn't overrun by parasitic rodents.

The more I pondered it the more I realized that the difference between human versus animal prey was that among animals there were clearly proscribed roles where predators were born and died predators and such was the same case among the prey. Whereas, among humans one could be born prey but could become a parasite as was currently the case.

We had allowed those who were meant to be prey to become a controlling class of parasites and it was not a role natural to them. Thus, they had taken that as an opportunity to go mishandle and made a devastating mess of things. They could no more lead as parasites anymore than a doe could in the wild. To do so would be unnatural and for that reason I began to see the urgency in the need for us to reclaim our position as predators. I saw how failing to do so had caused us to descend. We were living in an unnatural state.

As we pulled up to the house I began to feel lighter as the answers began to flood my mind. I began to see the world and my situation through a whole new lens. I no longer had to be ashamed of my new body. In fact, I began to see it as just the advantage that I needed to reclaim my status as predator and I was more ready than ever for the hunt.

16

I woke up the next morning feeling like a new woman. All night I had been brewing over all of the previous days' events.

"Well, you sure are beaming this morning," Doran observed.

"Yes I know. I guess you could say that I'm ready for the hunt. I've come to see my new body as an advantage. This skinsuit is the perfect camouflage!" I gleamed.

"Wow you seem to have had quite the epiphany last night! And you know what? You're absolutely right!" Doran replied.

"I know I am and now I'm ready to flip this thing back around. I can't really explain it either but I have what feels like a strong urge to hunt. I can taste it!" I added.

"Really, that's interesting that you say that because so do I! I've felt the urge ever since yesterday. It seemed like when that light bulb came on so did my predatory instincts. I'm feeling that same thirst," Doran confided.

"Really! Wow now I wasn't expecting you to say that! This is amazing. There is something different in the air today that's for sure. So do you think the others are feeling this too?" I asked.

"I do. What happened yesterday impacted us all. There's a reason we were all there. I believe that we are all experiencing the same thirst for the hunt, as you've described it. Don't worry we'll all meet again," Doran answered.

"I think you're right. I did feel a sense of connectedness with all of them. It was uncanny. I don't think I've ever felt anything like it. However, for as anxious as I am to hunt, I'm still pondering the how. I'm still not sure of the strategy. What about you?" I inquired.

"I've been thinking about that all night and I actually *do* have a strategy," Doran confidently replied.

He was always such a great thinker so I was anxious to listen as I sat on the edge of our bed putting on my socks anticipating the disclosure of his plans.

"You do!?! Ok, well spill it babe!" I commanded.

"Ok Mrs. Pushy! If you insist, I'll share," Doran said with a smirk. "What I've come up with is that we've got to get back to the basics. We've got to get back intuned with our natural selves."

"And what would our *natural selves* be?" I asked.

"Well naturally we are highly intuitive beings. In our natural state we have done things for which there has to this day been no scientific explanation nor any modern day technology that can replicate it. For instance, we built structures such as the pyramids, invented things that even today's most advanced technology can't replicate. That's because naturally we're beyond this world and we have to regain our connection with that part of ourselves," Doran explained.

"Hmmm.... I see and how are we supposed to do that? Especially given how far disconnected we are from that," I challenged.

"Well, it's about becoming the predator. We have to be strategic, focus and plan to get back in that state. We have to pursue the desire to do so like it is our prey. We have to become the ultimate predator in this hunt within the jungles of our minds. We have to avoid being so easily distracted and be in an almost blind pursuit of achieving this objective," Doran answered.

In that moment all I could do was gaze at him in awe. Frozen and speechless I thought, "Damn I love this man!"

"Baby, baby, baby! You are pure genius in physical form. I love your mind!" I shrieked, jumping up to hug him tightly.

"I love you too baby," Doran said squeezing me back.

"Ok, so now what specifically are you going to do to as the predator to tap into this natural intuitiveness? I'm so curious now!" I asked.

"Well that I'm going to have to intuit, no pun intended," Doran said with a light chuckle.

"Ok I see. You're right. That *is* the point right. Besides that it'll probably vary from person to person. Hmmmm.... well I guess it's hunting time. I need to locate my intuition," I said half jokingly.

"That's good, but the hunt is about going within *you* to locate it. It's not outside of yourself. And you have to be focused. No more distractions, specifically about your skinsuit. I believe that even that happened to distract you. It's also meant to give you an added challenge because it's forcing you to choose to be the predator versus the parasite," Doran advised.

"Now what do you mean by that," I queried.

"I mean that when this first happened you wanted to run and hide. You didn't want to go anywhere, but the natural response of a predator isn't to run. A predator stands it's ground and confronts the challenge. It's about honor for the predator. So I mean that you first have to deal with that part of things. Once you do that going within will be all the more easy," Doran offered.

"I see. You're absolutely right babe. I can't even deny that," I said looking a little less confident.

Doran was right and I knew it. I had some preparing to do before the hunt and I had to do it on my own. I was the one in the new skinsuit and I had to face it and look it in the eye without fear. It was time for me to choose to be the predator and stop being the parasitic rodent trying to hide my dirt in the darkness.

Doran went to go workout so I decided to do some yoga since Ina was still at a friend's. I got up, got dressed in my yellow, wide-legged, stretch yoga pants and a white v-neck tank and headed to our meditation room. On the way, I grabbed the vertical floor mirror from our master bathroom. I was finally ready to confront her.

17

When I got to the meditation room I positioned the mirror on the floor against the wall facing towards where I had planned to position my yoga mat. Then I rolled out my mat, lit a few white candles and a few sticks of frankincense. I decided that it was better to work in silence so I didn't put on my usual meditation/yoga music mix. I needed to focus and didn't want even the slightest distraction.

I sat on the mat then took a few deep, long inhalations and in what seemed like less than 60 seconds I was experiencing what could best be described as an out-of-body experience. At first it just seemed like I was just looking at myself from the outside where everything about me still felt normal. Then, just moments later I had a feeling of weightlessness. I felt like I was soaring above myself and looking down.

I looked down below and saw that it was more than just a feeling and I actually *was* floating! For a second I thought that I must have been tripping. I thought that I must have gone into a deep meditation and was just having a *serious* visualization. However, I knew that wasn't true because it was all way too real to be a visualization. I was really floating!

Then, just that fast I was consumed with a feeling of invincibility. I could fly!!! I could go anywhere I wanted to go. I could do anything that I wanted to do. I was free!

In my angst and at the moment of my thoughts of freedom I instantly began to take flight. I soared high above myself, my physical self, that is. I looked down upon my physical body with a bit of pity. I thought how sad it was to be trapped in that body, unable to experience the feeling of bliss that I was currently experiencing. Then I thought of how sad it was for everyone else who was trapped in those bodies.

Just then I wondered if this meant that I was dead. What I was experiencing seemed to be what many described in near death experiences. However, when I looked down at myself I saw that I wasn't dead, but was sitting there meditating in a deeply relaxed state. It was a weird sensation because I could actually still feel myself in my body. I could feel myself breathing. I could feel my heart beating. I still experienced all of the physical sensations of being in my body, but it just seemed that I did so as an observer.

I was stumped. Was this another stage of the change that my body was going through? Was I transforming yet again? I couldn't imagine what more could happen. I was already in a completely different body and now staring down at it. If I was transforming again I much prefered this transformation. I felt a weightlessness that I'd never before experienced. It was as if I hadn't a care in the world.

I began to embrace this feeling and the more I did the more free I felt. In that moment I let go of all emotion. Then the more I let go, the lighter I became. Soon I felt as light as a feather. I was no longer carrying the weight of all of my troubles and it felt so liberating.

I decided to venture out beyond my house to fully embrace my new found freedom. I flew everywhere. I still felt like myself, but lighter. It was like yet another version of myself had emerged. Then it seemed the more I let go of the cares of the world the lighter I became. It was a weightlessness that was before then unimaginable.

There were some moments that I wanted to visit all the places in the world that I wanted to see, but never got the chance to. However, just as fast as the thought came it escaped me because I became less and less concerned with the physical world. The desire to let go became more and more intoxicating and I was drunk with it.

So I let go until there was nothing more to hold on to. It was the most liberated I'd ever felt. Yet, the strange thing was I didn't feel anymore. It seemed that feeling had become an emotion that I then viewed as undesirable. Feelings seemed to be the thing that had all the time before kept me bound and separated from the heaven that I was then feeling inside. I couldn't imagine going back to that state. The mere thought of doing so was like being a prisoner.

Then I had an epiphany. This all began to feel so familiar. I wondered if I had been here before. It felt like home, almost as if I had come full circle. I began to crave more knowledge. I needed to know more about this aspect of myself. Who was I really? I needed the truth.

Then just as quickly as I asked the question I landed right back into my body. Again we were one. I was bound and weighted down and the bliss of what I had just moments prior been experiencing had come to a much dreaded end.

Yet, something had changed. I felt lighter still, even in my physical body. I still felt what I could only describe as a nothingness for the world. What was before such a big deal for me suddenly didn't seem all that serious. It was as if I knew that I had a bigger purpose and those petty issues were simply background noises that I began to discard.

It seemed that I had been in the meditation room for an eternity so I decided to get up and go see what Doran was up to. We never disturbed one another during meditation in the room, but I knew that I had been in there for far too long and probably had him worried so I wanted to go check in with him.

It seemed that I was right and that I *had* been in the meditation room forever because when I came out it was dark outside. I couldn't believe just how long I had been in there! I wondered why hadn't Doran come to get me? Did he pick Ina up? What the hell was going on?

18

I ran into our room to find that Doran was in the bed fast asleep bundled up under the covers the way he always did. I wondered why he hadn't come to get me. For a moment the thought crossed my mind again that perhaps I was dead. Maybe that out-of-body experience was more than just an out-of-body experience. However, before I could settle into the idea of that thought I saw the strangest thing. There was something very different about Doran. I moved closer to see if my eyes were deceiving me.

Then, as I approached him I got the shock of my life. The same feeling that I had when I woke up to find that I was in a different body was the same feeling that I experienced when I looked down on the bed to find that the same thing had happened to Doran.

In a panic I immediately and vigorously shook him awake. "Doran! Doran! Doran! Wake up!!!"

Jumping up he sat up in the bed and looked at me worried and said, "Baby, baby calm down. What's wrong?"

I didn't even know how to begin to tell him. Everything was wrong! It was like the invasion of the body snatchers, like we were in some alternate universe. I couldn't begin to tell him what was wrong because I had no idea what was happening myself. I wondered if it was the end of the world or something. It was like in one of those apocalyptic movies where all you see are white people. I always wondered about that. Why the hell are there never any black people in those movies? Do we all supposedly just disappear? I didn't have time to explore that theory. I had to focus on finding a way to break the news to Doran.

Knowing the deed had to be done I softly answered, "Babe, I really hate to say this, but I need for you to calmly look down at your hand. Please don't panic babe."

No sooner had I said that did Doran jump up with lightening speed and run to our bathroom to look in the mirror. Speechless, he looked in the mirror eyes bulging and hands touching his face as if trying to validate that his face was real.

"I know how you feel babe. I know," I said trying to comfort him. Just then I heard Ina at the door. Doran must have gone to pick her up after all. I guess he didn't want to disturb me in the mediation room.

"Mommy! Mommy! Something's wrong!" I heard Ina yell in a panic. In an instant Doran and I diverted our attention away from his dilemma to Ina. I ran to the door with Doran trailing close behind to see what was wrong. When I opened the door I got the shock of my life! Just when I thought I had seen it all and that things couldn't possibly get any stranger all things rational went out the window. In that moment there was no longer such a thing as rational. I began to question what was even real anymore.

As I opened the door wide what my eyes saw defied all ration. Ina, like Doran, had seemingly overnight gone through the same transformation that I had experienced several nights before. Watching their panic-stricken white faces staring back at me as if waiting for me to give them answers brought me all the way back into my own white body.

I had no idea what was happening. It felt more and more like something out of a movie. It just didn't feel real. Then again I had no idea what *real* even was anymore. For all I knew what I had always thought of as real wasn't.

Breaking the silence Ina asked with a look of panic, "Mommy, Daddy what's happening? I went to go use the bathroom and when I looked in the mirror I saw this," she said pointing to her now white face.

I couldn't believe my eyes. My once beautiful little caramel, doe-eyed, dimple-faced little girl had transformed into a blonde-haired, pale-faced, pink-lipped vanilla ghost.

Just then I thought aloud, "That's it! That's it babe!"

"What is it?," both Doran and Ina asked simultaneously.

"We're all becoming ghosts! At least sort of," I reasoned.

"Ghosts!" they both screeched.

"I don't feel like a ghost," Doran replied. "In fact, I feel very much alive. If I were a ghost I wouldn't be feeling like crap about being in this white skinsuit!" he continued with a hint of anger.

"Yeah mom! We're not dead!" Ina chimed in.

Moving over to sit on our bed I motioned for Doran and Ina to follow me so that I could explain.

"I don't mean ghost in the literal sense. It's just that I had an epiphany while I was meditating earlier. I felt like this body was a previous version of myself. It was like a lower form of me that existed before I went on to evolve into a higher self. It was mind-blowing. I mean it felt like I was floating on the clouds," I began to explain as they both looked at me more confused than ever and still panicked about their own situations.

"I know it sounds crazy, but these bodies are like hosts. We aren't meant to stay in them forever. I think that we are evolving," I continued.

"Evolving into what? A higher form? Are you saying these white bodies are a higher form than our black ones? What you're saying makes no sense," Doran said with a hint of irritation.

"Actually, what I'm saying is just the opposite. This transformation is our regression back to a lower form. It's like we've come full circle and are now on the verge of evolving into another, higher level of ourselves. I know that sounds crazy babe but its true. It's the truth I am realizing right now in this very moment. I don't even know how I'm coming up with this stuff. It's like I've been here before and this is all coming back to me now," I explained.

"So you think this is happening to all of us?" Ina asked.

"Yes baby, I do. In fact, I'd bet money on it," I answered. Then before I could complete my thought Doran's cell phone rang. I looked at the clock to see that it was 2:17am. I wondered who was calling him at that hour. He went to grab his phone from the dresser and then my cell phone rang. Doran and I looked at each other both wondering what was going on as we went to answer our phones.

I looked down at my phone and saw that it was Cre calling. I quickly answered, wondering if everything was okay with her. "Hey girl! Is everything alright?"

"Netty! Netty! Girl I turned white! I mean really! My ass is a white girl! I woke up to go to the bathroom, looked in the mirror and got the shock of my damn life! I don't know what is happening! This is some freaky shit! How the hell did this happen?" Cre yelled into the phone buzzing 90 miles a minute.

Interrupting I stopped her, "Cre I know. It's happening to all of us." I listened on the phone for her response and for a brief moment it was quiet enough to hear ants crawling as Cre processed what I had just told her.

"What do you mean girl? This happened to ya'll too!" Cre exclaimed.

"Yeah. It's happening all over the world. In fact, I'd bet that by now the world is probably white from the sounds of it. Seems that sometime this morning it happened while we slept. It actually happened to me about a week ago. I didn't tell anyone and Doran suggested I act like I'm some distant cousin by marriage visiting. So that's what I've been doing. I figured if I said anything to anyone else about it they'd think I was crazy. But we all went through the same shock that you're going through right now," I explained feeling that Cre was still in shock.

"Girl this is crazy. None of it makes sense. I think I must still be asleep and that I'll wake up in a little while to find that this is all a bad dream," Cre reasoned.

"I know it's difficult to accept, but this is real. You're not dreaming. You're evolving. We all are," I said hesitantly, not sure how deep to delve into the rabbit hole with Cre.

Cre was cool and my best friend, but she wasn't the most open-minded person I knew. So there were certain things that I just didn't share with her. In fact, the only one I'd ever discussed such things with was Doran. He and I were like-minded in that way. I could discuss anything with him no matter how outlandish it may seem to others. Doran got me.

Momentarily I listened on to hear that Doran was talking to our son, J. Seems J was discovering his new body as well and had called Doran for answers. The two of them were very close and would often have long discussions about metaphysics and consciousness so I wasn't surprised that J called Doran rather than me. He often sought Doran's advice and considered him to be his wise council.

I looked at Doran and shook my head silently letting him know that Cre was on the line experiencing the same dilemma. We both continued to counsel them as best we could in the midst of taking calls that started to pour in as our other lines buzzed. Everyone was calling. It was like they all needed to validate that what was happening to them individually was happening to all of us. We must have spent hours on the phone. Eventually, Ina had fallen back to sleep on our bed. Since we had a large king-sized bed she was able to stretch out in the middle and still sleep comfortably.

By about 6am the phones stopped ringing. Everyone had by then compared notes with enough people and were no doubt exhausted and coming down from the adrenaline rush of it all.

Then, as if things couldn't get any weirder.....

19

Exhausted from the morning's events Doran, Ina and I had all dozed off to sleep and were all sprawled out on the bed when we each jumped up simultaneously looking at each other in sheer amazement.

As we slept the strangest thing happened. The same thing that had happened earlier during my meditation had happened to all of us and we were all aware of it. There was a bright beam of light shining that scared us so that as fast as we left our bodies we returned. For the split second that we had done so we each looked around and saw one another looking down on ourselves. Yet, we were looking down on our physical bodies from our other bodies, which looked so strange that it scared us back into our white bodies.

"What the hell was that?" I asked Doran.

"I don't know, but I'm assuming you saw the same thing that I did when I looked at the two of you," he replied.

"Yeah, what the hell was that?" I inquired still in a state of shock.

Ina sat looking at both of us in silence no doubt as shocked as we were.

"I don't know, but it looked like a beam of light. It was so blinding that I couldn't even look at it directly.

I'm assuming that you too saw that same thing?" he inquired.

"Man that was crazy! I had a similar experience earlier when I was meditating. Well, at least the feeling of it was similar. I guess I didn't see what I just saw because it was just me. Wow! That was incredible. What does this mean? What is happening to us?" I asked Doran.

"Hmmm... I need a moment to digest it all. I'll be back," Doran said as he got up to leave the room.

Looking over at me Ina said, "I think I know what it is mom." As she spoke she looked at me intensely and knowingly as if she knew something that I didn't.

Ina often listened on as Doran and I engaged in long conversations concerning things of a metaphysical nature so I wondered if what she had to say was along those lines.

She paused before continuing on as if waiting to see how I would react.

"Oh wow Ina. Well, I'd love to hear your take on this. What are your thoughts?" I asked eager to hear.

It was so strange seeing my little girl in this strange body. It was even stranger hearing her speak the way that she did. There was something different in the way that she spoke to me. She suddenly seemed so much older and wiser than her years. As she spoke she took on a very mature tone. I almost forgot it was Ina who was speaking.

"We are all changing mom," she said blankly before pausing again while looking at me intensely.

Just then Doran came back into the room looking way more calm then when he had left carrying 3 bottles of water.

"What's going on?" he asked sensing the seriousness of the tone now dominating the room as he handed Ina and I a bottle of water.

"Ina has an idea about what's going on and she was just about to share her thoughts on it with me," I answered looking at Ina. "Go ahead and continue buttercup," I said.

"Mom and Dad we're changing, but not how you think. Our bodies are changing to a lower form. But then we have a spiritual body and it's turning into light. So we're like two people trying to become one and the more we let go and let it happen the lighter we'll be. But the more we hold on to what we were the more we'll be the lower form and we can get even lower than this. So we have to do something fast because if we don't we will get lower and lower and it'll be harder to get out. To get out we need a pure heart, all of us. We have to let go," Ina explained.

I couldn't believe my ears. Ina spoke with such intelligence that I momentarily forgot that she was just 10 years old. Doran apparently was thinking the same thing because he looked over at me with the same look of surprise.

"How do you know all of this," I inquired.

"You won't believe this, but this same thing happened in a show that I watch. It's a cartoon called "White Oblivion," Ina replied.

"Yeah I heard about that cartoon!" Doran exclaimed. "It's about the world turning white then all the people evolve into some type of angels. Salim and I were just talking about it. I thought it was interesting how they depicted themselves as us, if you know what I mean," Doran said looking at me matter-of-factly.

"Oh yeah, how come I haven't seen it yet? Guess I need to catch up. It's funny though because earlier when I had my little experience while meditating I was seeing how similar this all was to those apocalyptic movies where you don't see any black people. I guess that show you're talking about is similar," I responded.

"Yeah, but it's different, because in the show the people in the world don't exactly turn into white humans. They look more like an alien race of people who happen to be white," Ina clarified.

"Yeah she's right. You could say that they were light beings. In fact, a lot like what we all just saw when we we looked at one another," Doran added.

"Hmmm so you're saying that we are an alien race?" I asked shocked by what I was hearing.

"No mom, we're not aliens. We're just sort of.... evolving. That's the best way to explain it," Ina said.

Just then we heard someone come through the front door. Doran looked at Ina and I then smiled knowing who it was.

Then I heard a familiar voice. "Mom, Dad, Ina! I'm here!"

It was J. He must have taken the first flight out to make his way home. In all of the commotion I hadn't gotten a chance to ask Doran how J was dealing with everything.

Ina and I quickly jumped up and trailed behind Doran making our way to the living room. We all looked at J and he looked at us strangely as our changed appearances made it difficult to express the joy that we would have normally expressed during such a homecoming.

"Peace son!" Doran said hurrying to greet J eagerly.

J's changed appearance didn't at all affect Doran's joy. We hadn't seen J in over 6 months and Doran more than any of us seemed so excited to have him return home.

"Peace Dad!" J said hugging Doran.

Ina and I ran up and hugged him also until we were all in a group hug. It was so good to have J home. Though it was just as weird seeing J the way he was he still felt very much like my son.

It was funny because though Doran wasn't J's biological father, in our white skinsuits they looked more like father and son than they did before. They were both tall, broad-shouldered, brunettes with the whole 5 o'clock shadow beard thing going. It was so funny to see.

"So have you all figured out what's going on? Everybody is talking about it. It's all I heard on the plane ride here. Have you all been out yet? The whole world is white now. I mean the whole world! They're saying it's like a scene out of some cartoon called "White Oblivion." Have you all heard of it?" J asked

We each looked at him and laughed.

"Yeah, Ina was just filling us in on that. Apparently it's some new kids show that's out. But how does something from someone's imagination in a kids show end up being our reality? That must be one hell of a show!" I exclaimed.

"Well people are all saying that the writer for that show is a black woman who is apparently one hell of a channeler. Her name is..... Connie.." J said before Doran chimed in.

"Murphy!" Doran said completing J's sentence.

"Yeah! How did you know?" J asked.

"We just attended an event where she spoke on this whole phenomenon. But I had no idea that she had anything to do with that show. Hmmmm very interesting," Doran said deep in thought looking like his mind was racing.

"Yeah, apparently she has become one heavily sought after woman. The government and the media is trying to track her down now to try to get some answers," J continued.

"Well I doubt they're gonna find her. She probably doesn't want to be found. This is rather interesting though because at the event that we went to she told us that we would be reverting back to our true selves. I had no idea that this is what she meant," Doran said before looking over at me. "What about you baby, did you picture this as what she was saying?"

"Not by a long shot. This is crazy. But you know after hearing what you've all just told me and remembering what Connie said about the whole predator, prey thing I see that the hunt is on because now we have the best camouflage ever," I sneered.

"Not only does this skinsuit level the playing field, but it more clearly defines our roles. It makes clear who the true parasites of the world are. It eliminates the distraction of racial issues and forces us as the natural predators that we are to go within and figure this out. Once the dust from this settles we'll come into our true form. We won't have to any longer deal with our black boys being murdered by cops. We won't be distracted by our own internal divisions such as black man versus black woman, light skin versus dark skin and all the other nonsense we waste our time obsessing over. We can start to focus on what matters, which is our evolution. Like Ina said, what this is is our evolution. We are evolving and it's happening this way so that we do," I further explained.

"You're absolutely right about that," Doran agreed.

"So now what? I mean what happens now?" J asked as if directing his question toward all of us.

"Hmmm... Good question J and at the moment that is the million dollar question," Doran responded.

"Well for now I'd say we need to eat something so I'm gonna make my way into the kitchen to whip us up something. What about your favorite breakfast J?" I asked smiling at my sorely missed son.

"Oh wow! That sounds perfect Ma," J gleamed.

I got up to give J another big hug. I missed him so much! Having him back home was the only answer I needed for now. Ina seemingly felt the same way. She sat cuddled close to J interlocking her arm with his as if to make sure he wouldn't get away.

Looking up at him she smiled and said, "I missed you too J! I'm glad you're home."

Smiling back at her J said, "I missed you too lil sis!"

It was great to have our family together again even with all that was going on. Beaming ear to ear I skipped into the kitchen to whip up J's favorite breakfast which consisted of veggie sausage patties, biscuits, home fried potatoes with a side of fried apples. He always loved a big breakfast. Usually I only fixed all of that when I was in the mood to do so because there was so much to prepare, but that time I was eager to do so. Having J home was definitely a special enough occasion.

As the scent of J's favorite breakfast began to fill the air they all started to make their way into the kitchen to check on the status of things.

"Ummm mmph baby! Smelling good in here. What are we looking like? Do you need for me to do anything? I can get the plates if you like," Doran offered.

With a chuckle I responded, "Yes sure babe you can do that. Can you also pour us each something to drink. Except you can skip mine because I'm having tea."

"Sure thing my love," Doran replied smiling back.

You could tell that he was so happy to have J back at home. The two of them had been talking nonstop since I got to the kitchen. It seemed they had so much to catch each other up on.

"You know J just said the most profound thing. He was telling me some more about this great search for Connie Murphy. He told me that the last sighting of her was reported to be 6 months ago. So I was telling him that that couldn't be true because we just saw her at the event the other night. I just thought that was very weird though. I guess no one from the event disclosed her whereabouts. My guess is that she doesn't want to be found. I'm glad we got to see her though and that she gave us the heads up on what was to come. Though I had no idea that it would actually happen this way and especially not this fast," Doran filled me in.

"Yeah that *is* weird," I said looking perplexed.

When Doran left back out of the kitchen to return to the living room with the others I was deep in thought wondering about Connie. That *was* very weird. I also thought that she was acting rather weird on the day of the event. First of all, that was the shortest lecture ever. I'm sure several others was expecting more. Also, I thought that it was strange that she hadn't really even covered her prepared presentation. I guess ultimately she ended up doing exactly what she was supposed to do so I left it at that.

Finally, breakfast was ready so I called the family to come into the kitchen to eat. Doran had taken the liberty of setting the table while he was in the kitchen so all I had to do was furnish the table with the food.

I had just put the final dish on the table and before I could blink twice everyone was there. Doran sat on one side of me and Ina on the other leaving a space for J to sit on the side adjacent to me.

"Ummmm smells like black people food up in here Ma just like I remember. Man have I missed this!" J exclaimed taking in a forkful of potatoes.

"Yeah I'm sure you don't get food like this in Colorado," I joked.

We all sat down and moments later everyone was digging in.

Then shortly after the grubbing down silence Doran broke the silence and said, "So son tell me more about what it's like out there in the world right now. Did the white people seem to know anything?"

"That's just it dad you can't tell who 'the white people' are versus the blacks. Only in situations like this where you were expecting me would you know who was who," J replied.

"Hmmmm that is just what I thought. My how the tables have turned," Doran answered shaking his head.

I knew just what he meant too and he was absolutely right. The tables had indeed turned and I couldn't help but wonder just what the implications of that would be. I was sure that we'd all find out sooner rather than later.

20

The rest of the day of J's homecoming was a joy. We were all so happy to have him back that for a moment we hadn't even dealt with the matter at hand. However, the next morning was a different story.

When I woke up Doran appeared to be deep in contemplation.

With a look of concern as I open my eyes from what was actually a very good night's sleep I asked, "Wow what's so heavy on your mind this early in the morning babe?"

"What's *not* on my mind? With everything that's happened I can't stop thinking about it all. What this means for us? How this changes things? What our next steps need to be? What our choices are now? I mean the list could go on. We all have a lot to think about," he replied.

"Yeah I understand that. I've wondered the same thing. I don't think we'll really know until we go out and see for ourselves how things are now. We've kind of been in here since it all happened so we don't really know the state of affairs just yet," I answered.

"Exactly and I'm itching to find out. I was actually planning to do just that today," Doran continued.

"That's a good idea. Ironically, I actually want to go out myself to see how things are. It's funny though because when it first happened to me the last thing I wanted to do was go out and now it's all that I can think about. Well I'm ready whenever you are babe. This is going to be something to see." I gleamed.

"It's going to be more than just something to see. This is a total game changer! Life as we knew it is no more and I for one am anxious to see how my new life will unfold!" Doran explained.

Just then there was a knock on our bedroom door.

"Come on in," Doran instructed.

"Morning! Rise and shine!" J greeted seemingly gliding into the room as he first headed toward my side of the bed to kiss me on the cheek.

"You're sure in a good mood," I observed leaning over to make my cheek available.

"It is indeed. Hell this is the best day of all of our lives. The playing field is officially even and I can't wait to see just how even it is!" J gleamed.

"You got that right son!" Doran chimed in.

"So what's the plan Dad? Where we heading to first?" J asked.

With a brief snicker, Doran replied, "Hmmm... I don't know. There are just so many places I'd like to start with. It's hard to pick."

Laughing along J replied, "Yeah exactly! I'd like to go to a bank and ask for a loan. Or maybe we should apply for housing or a high-paying job for an exec position that doesn't do a damn thing all day but take all the credit for everyone else's hard work!"

We all laughed at that one.

"Maybe I should be a groupie and go hang around the football and basketball players," I added.

Doran and J got quiet.

"I'm just kidding guys. You gotta admit that black celebrities and athletes *do* kinda act like white women are the shit and whatnot. Guess it gives them a sense of accomplishment," I said half jokingly.

"Yeah well that's how it is. It was all part of the programming that we bought into some time ago. Never thinking that we were good enough. I want to see how that plays out now," Doran replied.

"So when are we doing this dad? You ready to get into the mix and see how things are out there?" J asked.

"Damn right. Was just about to get dressed now," Doran responded getting up and heading toward our bathroom.

A few minutes later anxious to check things out Doran and J had quickly gotten dressed and decided to take a walk around the neighborhood while Ina and I got ready for us to all go sightseeing together.

21

The cool, crisp Fall air swept through Doran and J like an ocean wave. "Wow that feels good!" Doran shouted taking in a deep breath just after stepping outside and shutting the door behind him.

"Yeah, cold air is like an entirely different experience in this white skinsuit," J said jokingly.

"Guess we have to get used to this. You're right though. Ordinarily I'd hate this cold weather, but now it feels almost refreshing," Doran replied.

"So where are we heading first J? Though from the looks of things we may not need to go far. Check that out," Doran said pointing to a white couple dancing in the streets about a block away. "I guess it's safe to say they're happy about the change of events."

"Yeah, dad there's a lot of that going on. It's a whole new world out here now. A lot of happy people out there. Though there are a fair share of unhappy people out there also. We're not all happy about this. In fact, I would say it's pretty split down the middle," J informed.

"Yeah, I'm probably with that bunch. This is hardly something to be happy about. However, I can understand why some would think that it was. For so long we've been ostracized because of our dark skin. Now not having to deal with that is certainly a plus. However, I'm more interested in *why* this is happening, what's to come and what we are all gonna do about it. There is obviously a bigger reason for this and we have to get focused on figuring out what that is," Doran said.

"I agree dad. That's why I came home. I also know that sooner or later those among the real white folks will respond. We have to be ready for that. They're a very arrogant people and I doubt they see this as a good thing. In fact, happy wasn't at all the response that I observed on the trip here. The white folks were so irate over it that it's actually what made them identifiable," J explained.

"So are you saying that you think things are gonna get ugly? Should we be preparing?" Doran asked.

"That's exactly what I'm saying dad. I know what I saw in their eyes and in my opinion this white skinsuit is hardly anything to celebrate. Besides that the ones of us who aren't happy are on the extreme end of the spectrum of unhappiness. That being the case, I really don't know how this is gonna turn out," J added.

"Hmmm, that's very interesting J," Doran began before being interrupted by a loud crashing sound. Doran and J ran up the street toward the noise to see what happened.

They arrived about 2 blocks away to see a blonde-haired guy standing outside of his car yelling furiously at the homeowners of a house that he had crashed his car into. The husband, a tall, dark-haired slender man who owned the home was pacing frantically trying with all that he had in him to calm down to keep from attacking the car owner. The wife was diligently attending to her husband pleading with him not to kill the driver.

However, despite the wife's efforts to keep her husband from attacking the man it seemed the driver was egged on by the husband's restraint, which only worsened the situation. Feeling a false sense of security in his own arrogance the driver kept mouthing off and stomping around, though cautiously enough to remain near his car.

Recognizing the house as that of a familiar neighbor and home of a good friend of Ina's, Doran cautiously approached the couple saying, "Charles? Is that you?"

With a hint of relief in having heard a familiar voice the husband responded, "Yeah man I'm Charles. Is that you Doran?"

"Yeah man it's me," Doran greeted going to dap Charles' hand. "Hey what happened here? What's going on?" he inquired.

"Man this fool just ran his car into my house. I got my family in here and whatnot. We just happened to all be upstairs at the time so no one got hurt, but man this is my house and this cracker fool lost his damn mind! Then he still mouthing off! These crackers are gettin too comfortable! I mean man when they start just doin what they want like ain't gone be no consequences I got a real problem with that. They getting way too comfortable man!"

"Oh I know, I know man. They are. Why don't you send the queen in the house while we deal with this out here," Doran offered saying what wasn't being said aloud with his eyes.

Meanwhile, the driver was still stomping around shouting all types of obscenities while talking to someone on his cell phone.

Charles said something privately to his wife and she turned, half-smiled, waved at Doran and J then went back into the house.

"So do you know this dude?" Doran asked Charles.

"Naw man, I don't know him," Charles answered calmly before abruptly and unexpectedly turning to charge the driver.

Within about 5 seconds Charles had charged the driver. "Man ya'll gettin way too comfortable! This is my house and I got my family in there! What the fuck is wrong with you fool," Charles yelled in between blows. Charles was beating the man relentlessly.

Doran and J ran up to stop Charles. It took all the strength that both of them had to pull Charles off of the man.

"Come on man. He ain't worth all that. Plus we got another way to handle this man. Not here. Not like this. Too much going on right now. Come off him man," Doran pleaded looking around at the huge crowd of people that had formed.

Just then Doran spotted me working my way through the crowd to get to him. "Doran what's going on here?" I said panic-stricken trying to quickly assess the scene.

"Baby it's fine. We got it. Go back home. I don't want you out here. Where is Ina? You need to get back to her," Doran ordered.

I knew not to question him so I quietly made eye contact with him to assure him that I understood and went back to the house.

I'd gotten a frantic call from Kim, Charles' wife, that she was afraid that Charles, Doran and J were going to do something terrible and that I needed to get to her house right away. I didn't know what was going on so I immediately headed down to her house. I had no idea that some man had rammed his car into their house. When I saw what had happened I knew, and apparently better than she did, that an act like that was gonna be dealt with through street justice and I wasn't about to get in the way of that. I knew better to leave that to the brothahs, in white skinsuits and all. The skinsuits didn't change who we were as black folks who stayed true to a certain code.

About an hour later I heard Doran and J walk through the door. I was anxious to hear how things turned out and was just about to ask them about it. However, something came on the tv interrupting Ina's cartoons that instantly caught my attention. It was unheard of for a news broadcast to interrupt a cable network channel, especially a children's channel at that.

I grabbed the remote from the tv stand just as Doran and J were walking into the family room both taking seats to see what was being reported.

The news reporter was saying that the police and military forces were being called into the inner cities to barricade the borders for what they claimed were safety reasons. She went on to report that the CDC was going to be testing those of us who had transformed into white people to see what was going on. Thus, the government was urging everyone who was among those people to immediately report to the nearest CDC clinic for testing.

Doran, J and I looked at one another knowing full well that the barricades and 'testing' had nothing to do with keeping anyone safe.

Given the history between people of color and others there was no doubt in our minds that the barricades were more for identification purposes. They wanted to be still be able to identify who was who and because most of the residents of the inner cities were people of color the barricades were their way of keeping us separate from them. They needed to stall while they figured out a way to maintain power.

However, in their arrogance the parasites failed to see that we had been one in the same all along. The more time I spent in my white skinsuit the more I came to realize this. I wasn't any less of who I'd always been because of the skin change. Soon we would all realize that.

The immaturity of our oppressors to think any differently was a display of their own innate childish nature. Yet, we were an ancient people who knew better than to adopt such childish beliefs.

As Doran and Connie had concluded we had adopted the ways of prey. We had convinced ourselves to trade places with those who were the true prey who later transformed into parasites. In doing so we strayed far from who we were inherently and so the barricades were put into place to protect them from us once we remembered this.

I sat gazing at the tv screen after the news report had gone off swept away with my own thoughts.

"So now we're on lockdown. I guess that's why the white guy rammed his car into Charles' house. I'm sure there's a lot of people going off. More than that I bet all the white people in the city are going off cause they ain't used to being boxed in," Doran said.

Yeah and I bet they're *really* petrified about being trapped in here with us!, "I added.

"Well that's what they get. They wanted to take DC back didn't they. Now they got just what they wanted," J said half-jokingly.

"Well this certainly changes things. The world as we knew it is gone for sure and I see they're using this whole situation to enforce martial law. However, as usual their response is counter-productive and with all their so-called intelligence they're too dumb to see that," Doran chimed in again.

"What do you mean by that babe?" I asked.

"You'll soon see," he replied and with that Doran went into the kitchen to wash his hands and grab a glass of water.

22

Over the next several weeks a lot had changed. For starters, no one was being permitted to go in or out of the major cities or anywhere else that was primarily occupied by blacks.

That meant that for blacks the whole going to work thing had virtually become obsolete. No one was really working unless they were one of the ones who had a business within the barrier, particularly businesses selling goods that were basic necessities.

So if you owned a gas station you were still in business as well as a grocery store owner. Businesses like mine and Doran's had taken a hit. No one was in the mood nor had the resources to spare for yoga classes.

Doran wasn't able to make any of his booked photo shoots. What he did instead was take a more journalistic approach to his craft often going out and shooting images of the white-washed world. His photos were definitely telling a story. A few of them he was able to sell to newspapers and magazines.

Since a lot of people within the barriers could not get to work a large community of people had started to barter. The lockdown made it very difficult to get the basic necessities. There weren't a lot of stores in the inner cities and the military was not allowing any supply trucks to pass through. All of this meant that food and other resources were quickly becoming scarce.

We had always been quite the frugal ones so considering everything we actually weren't doing too bad. Having been a single mom for so long I had always been an extreme couponer and stayed prepared for anything.

So I always kept a fully packed pantry. You name it we had loads of it. The only thing that we were short on were fresh, whole foods which were a large part of our diet as vegetarians. Nonetheless, I made the best of what we had which were plenty of canned and dried beans, rice, frozen tofu, canned mock chicken and veggies, a freezer full of frozen veggies, flour, nuts and seeds and dried fruit.

We still ate quite sparingly than usual in order to make our supplies last.

We were however, growing increasingly more concerned about the utilities going out soon so Doran suggested I start getting used to cooking on the grill. Meanwhile, he and J were stockpiling water. They would go out and collect as many empty jugs and bottles that they could find.

Alot of those among us who were originally black actually started to really come together. Unlike how things were previously where we were always so divided and acting like crabs in a barrel robbing and stealing from one another we were actually helping one another out and ensuring that every family had what they needed.

At first there was a high incidence of robberies and the drug addicts were out of control becoming enraged and desperate for a fix once they ran out of drugs and pharmaceuticals to make more. However, before they got too out of hand other brothahs like Doran banned together to get them clean and back on track. Within no time the black community was tighter than ever. I figured that if barricading us in was supposed to be a test that we failed, then the examiner must have been sorely disappointed because we were definitely winning.

Doran said that whatever the plan was it was like all the others, a total bust so in the end none of it mattered. He said that in all of this our focus needed to remain on us and our own evolution.

So that's what we focused on, all of us. A lot of others thought just like Doran and so there was a general consensus throughout the community. Thus, we focused on ourselves and continued to evolve.

Though what followed was yet another very strange phenomenon.

23

We had been barricaded in for months and by then it was dead of winter. Most of the resources had run out. However, luckily we were all still bartering to make do.

Our utilities had been shut off so we were using the water that we had stockpiled very sparingly. I was cooking the meals on a wood-burning stove, which doubled as our heat source, that Doran had bartered in exchange for a couple of our chairs.

Doran and J had done a pretty good job sealing the windows so the house stayed fairly warm. As for electric, some of the brothahs had invented some way to still get it. Also, they'd cut off our access to cell phone towers and internet. Nonetheless, some of the tech savvy brothahs had devised something for that as well, which allowed us to access it for short periods of time throughout the day.

By then the military had gotten a lot more aggressive because hardly no one turned themselves into the CDC for 'testing.' That was probably because we all knew that the so-called 'request' to do so was a bunch of bull. Moreover, we knew that if we turned ourselves in that would have been the last that anyone would ever again see or hear from us.

There had already been several reports that many among us had come up 'missing.' Of course the media tried to put a negative spin on it saying that a lot of black men were folding under the pressure and abandoning their families. We knew that was a lie. They were kidnapping our men as an attempt to weaken us. It was an old tired play that had been played many times before.

So suffice it to say that things began to get very tense throughout the city. Collectively we started to band together more. Though we had to because there were more and more reports of military, police and government violence against us.

With regards to the actual white people who remained inside of the barrier with us it seemed the government had decided to sacrifice the many for the few because they weren't given any passes either.

Meanwhile, life went on as usual for the actual whites in other parts of the world where they were the majority. Oddly enough, blacks tended to stay close so it wasn't too difficult to barricade us in.

I often thought that interesting especially given our history of division. For centuries, Christians blacks disliked muslim blacks, light-skinned blacks disliked dark-skinned black, black men disliked black women, West Indian blacks didn't like American blacks. This list of division among us was endless. Though, with all the division that existed among us we still managed to somehow stay within close proximity of one another.

To me that said a lot. It meant that deep down we still had love for one another. Thus, I knew that when the time came that we needed to band together we would. There was an unseen force, a certain magnetism that would not allow us to separate and that to me was the true source of our power.

Meanwhile, the longer they had us barricaded in the stronger we became. Like many things in nature there was an unseen power in our numbers. It was likely the reason that there had always been so many agendas to keep us divided in the first place. Thus, the very thing that Doran eluded to when the barricades were first put up was exactly what happened.

Then, like the initial transformation, I was the first to experience the next phenomenon. It happened one evening after dinner while we were all in the living room. I was talking to Doran and J while Ina was deeply engrossed in a book. The next thing I knew Doran looked at me and though I could see his lips moving I couldn't hear any sound come out. Then in what seemed like an instant I noticed Doran, Ina and J staring at me with expressions of shock.

Startled I yelled, "What's wrong?"

No one answered and they all just stared at me open-mouthed and wide-eyed. It seemed that they couldn't hear any sound coming from my mouth anymore than I could from them.

Within seconds my own attention was diverted from them to myself. To my own disbelief I was levitating. However, it wasn't my white self, but my original self. I was me and I was levitating and sort of glowing. Besides that something felt different. It was a familiar feeling like the feeling I had that day at the time of my meditation experience. I felt lighter than usual, almost as light as a feather one could say.

Then in my peripheral I noticed something strange so I turned my head to the side and saw that I had wings! I actually had wings!!! Suddenly, no sooner had I noticed that did I experience the most overwhelming feeling of euphoria. I felt the most intense feeling of peace. I was sort of devoid of any emotion. It was almost as if all feelings, including emotions had been weighing me down and I was finally free.

I looked down at Doran then Ina and J and I felt love, pure love. It was a love unlike anything I had ever before experienced. It was a knowing, not a feeling. It wasn't the feeling of love that we experience as emotion.   It was love in it's purest form and it was intoxicating. I closed my eyes and as I did I could feel myself ascend higher.

Before long I blacked out. I had no memory of what happened during that time. When I awakened I was back on the couch as my white self. Doran, Ina and J were all hovering over me trying to shake me awake. I opened my eyes and smiled at them.

"Wow mom! What was that?" Ina winced. I could tell that whatever it was had frightened the daylights out of her.

"I don't know Ina what did you see and why are you all hovering over me?" I asked sitting upright.

"You were.... you were.... floating mom!" Ina said as if still in disbelief.

"Yeah and you were you again. Well at least kind of. You weren't exactly like you though. You had wings," J added with hesitation as if afraid to speak the words aloud.

"I know I saw it too. I was there," I said trying to add some humor to lighten the mood.

Doran sat quietly taking it all in before breaking his silence, "I know what's happening. We're coming into another stage of evolving. It's speeding up so what just happened to you briefly will soon be what happens to all of us permanently. Everything that has happened to you thus far has happened to all of us. We are returning to our original form and *that's* what they're afraid of. They're afraid that they'll no longer exist. Originally they weren't here. So it all makes perfect sense now," Doran explained as we each listened intently.

"You're exactly right dad!" J chimed in. "The man who drove the car into the Johnson's house was shouting something strange that eluded to that. He said, "You're one of them. I know you! I know you!" At the time I just thought he was some crazed white man angry about no longer being perceived as the ones in power. But that wasn't it at all. They knew who we were this whole time. Now it's over for them and they know exactly what's happening. But how did they know before we did?"

"That's a good question J. I have no idea. But it's no secret that they stole and thoroughly studied much of our ancient text, which predicted a lot of this. It's what gave them the upper hand all of this time. It's how they manipulated us into trading places with them," Doran continued to explain.

"Yeah you're right baby I definitely believe that. However, now that we're coming into remembering who we are what does that mean for us? What happens now? What are we gonna do with these newly remembered memories, so to speak?" I probed.

"That too is a good question and the way that I see it we have a choice between making this place a more suitable place to stay, minus the parasitic control or we destroy it and start over fresh. To me it's really that simple," Doran answered.

"In theory that sounds pretty accurate especially if we evolve into who our ancient text says we are... but what if we regress instead like your girl Connie said at that workshop you were telling me about?" J questioned.

"Well son if that happens then we're screwed anyway because we would have gone backwards rather than forward and we would have played right into their hands. That's what they want us to do. That's what the barricades, the martial law, the police brutality, the injustices. They're doing all of this to push our buttons to make us regress, but its time we stop giving them what they want. It's time we turn the tides. The brothahs and the sistahs just need to get on the same page about whatever the plan is because either way you spin it things are changing and their changing quickly.

Those who aren't on board will just get left. It's time to wake up. They got no love for us and every chance they get they try and destroy us. Yet time and time again we keep sparing them. We've had plenty of opportunities to take them, yet our own division so clouded in backstabbing, mistrust and self-hatred has prevented us from taking that shot when we've had it," Doran responded sternly.

"I feel you on that dad. But this time is different. All that they've done this time is make us tighter than ever. The old divide and conquer play ain't gon work this round. So now I guess they figure they gon just get gangsta and take us. So that means we gon have to get gangsta and street justice is gon have to prevail over those who ain't down. I mean look around... things aren't getting any better. So why aren't we doing anything now dad? What are we waiting for? They made a move and we're just sitting here," J said getting more worked up.

"I hear you son, but things have to be done at the right time and in the right way. It ain't time to respond and we're not ready. You think brothahs sitting around cool seeing their babies starving? You think brothahs are cool watching their queens suffering. This ain't okay son by any means, but acting prematurely ain't gonna do nothing but put us all at a much worse disadvantage. Son you gotta always consider the bigger picture and from all angles. Some big moves *are* about to be made and we're probably only gonna have one shot at this, which means we have to do things the right way," Doran explained.

Ina and I sat quietly listening to Doran and J planning and philosophising. They could go on that way for hours. I did so enjoy seeing Doran hand down his wisdom to J though. As a single mom wise counsel from a male perspective was never something that I could offer J. So when Doran came along it was a godsend.

24

Around 3am the next morning there was a banging on our door. Half asleep Doran and I looked at one another as if wondering if the other knew who it could be.

Doran got up to go see who was at the door as did I after putting on my robe. Having heard the knocking from his room in the basement J had come upstairs to see who it was also. Doran went to look through the peephole with J and I trailing closely behind.

Then, abruptly turning around Doran signaled for me to go get Ina and go to our room. Meanwhile, he and J stood by the door giving each other eye signals.

Quickly I ran upstairs to retrieve Ina then took her into our room as Doran had ordered. I then came back to the top of the stairs to see who was at the door. Doran opened the door and there two policemen who looked like they were SWAT or something. I wondered why they were knocking on our door

"Good evening sir. How's it going?" One of the cop's said.

"What can I do for you?" Doran replied calmly.

I noticed that J was not around so I figured that Doran must have told him to go hide somewhere.

"There have been quite a few disturbances reported. I'm sure you've been seeing the news by now and are aware of what's been going on. So we're just going around checking things to make sure things don't get out of hand," the cop answered.

"Oh well actually I'm fine here. I didn't report anything. In fact, I was just about to sit down for lunch," Doran responded.

"Oh are you here alone?" the other cop asked surprised.

Then before Doran could respond, the other cop interrupted and asked, "Mind if we take a look? From our experience you can't be too careful. We've had reports of people hiding out. Even had quite a few kidnappings."

The truth was there hadn't been any such reports. In fact, things were totally to the contrary. The community was tighter than ever and doing everything in it's power to avoid giving the cops an excuse to harass us. As for the kidnappings we had begun hearing some talk of that. Though it was suspected that the cops and military were the ones doing the kidnapping. It seemed that anyone who hinted at being any type of organizer was suddenly coming up missing. So for that reason, Doran and others like him were taking care to lay low.

It was clear that the cops were up to something. Somehow they had to come to view Doran and the rest of us a threat and it looked like they were there to see that we too came up 'missing.'

My mind started racing. I had to do something. There was no way I was going to let them take Doran or the rest of us. I knew Doran's plan was to sacrifice himself so that we could get away safely, but there was no way I was about to lose the love of my life.

Still maintaining a calm demeanor Doran responded to the cop saying, "I do mind. As I told you nothing to report here and I was just about to have a bite to eat. I *have* seen the news, but as I'm sure *you* know this neighborhood has been pretty quiet so I think I'm all good here officers. I do feel better knowing that you all are on the job though so thanks for stopping by now," Doran said waving and moving to close the door.

Just then one of the cops stuck his foot in the door while the other grabbed hold of his holster posturing to force his way in. Suddenly, I had a flashback of what happened to the black guy outside of Everlasting Life Cafe the day I had my first date with Doran. I saw a flash of every black boy the cops had brutally and maliciously murdered that year.

It was happening again, but this time they were walking right up to our doors and doing it. I refused to allow Doran to be one of those statistics! I remembered that Doran had stashed lots of weapons throughout our house as if expecting something like this to happen. So I stood up to go grab a couple planning to go help Doan when suddenly I was grabbed from behind.

25

I quickly turned my head to find that J had grabbed me from behind, covered my mouth and was dragging me into our room with Ina, who looked terrified.

Whispering J said, "Ma, Ina we have to get out of here. I need you to stay calm and do as I say. We gotta climb outta here onto the roof. We'll have to go this way," he said pointing to the window near where we were standing. "Those cops will be up here any minute so we don't have time to discuss it. I need you both to just do as I ask," he continued.

Ina and I didn't need any convincing. We could feel the tension in the air. Besides that I knew that Doran had instructed J to get us out of the house so I obeyed. I also knew that Doran, even with his calm demeanor, was prepared to defend his family at all cost and that he wanted to ensure that we were safe knowing that he didn't do so in vain.

Quickly, Ina went first onto the window ledge and quiet as a mouse J hoisted her up onto the roof. He went next. Meanwhile, I couldn't help but eavesdrop on what was going on downstairs. However, I could barely hear anything from the room with the door closed.

Then just as it was my turn as I stepped out onto the window ledge to grab J's hand from above for him to lift me up the most horrific of sound pierced my ears. It sent a sharp pang shooting through my heart like a poisonous arrow.

I heard a loud crack then Doran scream out in agonizing pain! It sounded like someone slammed a metal folding chair shut. However, I knew we didn't have any metal folding chairs and that the cracking sound was Doran's bones.

Breath instantly left my body and I was frozen. Still whispering, J frantically pled with me to come on. Overcome with despair my body went limp and J hung onto my arm with all of the strength that he could muster up.

I saw Ina peer over the roof ledge pleading with her eyes for me to please join them. I gathered some courage, got myself together and snapped out of it. Then, grabbing the roof ledge with one hand and holding onto J's hand with the other I hoisted myself up onto the roof.

When I climbed all the way up onto the roof J and Ina hugged me tightly. Ina had tears streaming down her face with her eyes plagued with terror. I was shaking like a leaf terrified at the thought of what they were doing to Doran.

In that moment I felt like life had left my body. Doran was my air. I had such a strong connection to him that it felt like I was experiencing his pain.

I couldn't believe how quickly things had taken a turn for the worst. My thoughts were racing and all that I could think about was what to do to save Doran. I wondered if I could make my wings come back and fly to his rescue and bring him back to safety. However, I had no idea how to make it happen. I knew that I had to do something, but I didn't know what that was. My heart was heavy with pain and I was struggling to focus enough to recall what was going on when it happened the first time to make it happen again. I needed my wings!

Then, just as the thought of it entered my mind I realized what it was. When I was levitating my heart was light!

Quickly I let go of all emotion. I allowed myself to feel that pure love that I felt when I was levitating. Before I knew it I was back. I'd done it! My wings had returned. Ina and J stared at me in awe.

I couldn't believe that I was able to invoke the shift on command. However, I had no idea how to get back into the house and even if I did I had no idea what I would do once I was in there. Then, just as quickly as I had shifted back into myself I was back into my white body.

I was devastated! I had failed Doran who loved me enough to risk his life for me! I was so upset with myself for not being able to hold it together long enough to help him in his time of need. Disappointment didn't begin to describe what I felt about myself in that moment. My worry over Doran had apparently been stronger than my love love for him and I felt horrible about that.

As I sulked J motioned for Ina and I to be still and quiet. The more I heard Doran's agonizing screams the harder I cried. I had to do something. I couldn't just keep hiding out on the roof while those monsters killed my husband.

I decided to give it another shot. However, the more I heard him scream the more hatred claimed my soul. I hated who they were. All they ever did was bring chaos and terror everywhere they went. Parasites all of them! I cursed their entire existence! It angered me how patient we'd always been with them and their childish, savagery ways.

All they ever did was kill and terrorize us and without ever having reason or justification for doing so. Meanwhile, we just stood by and let them do it. Why!?!?!?!!!

We were the ones with ample reason and justification to eliminate them, yet we never did. Always the passive, so-called 'peaceful' ones. The more these thoughts ran through my mind, more heated I became. I mean literally! The roof started to get really hot, which was strange because it was late Fall.

J looked at me and I looked over at him in puzzlement. It wasn't me causing things to heat up.

"What's happening?" I whispered.

"I'm not sure, but now we have to get off of this roof before we burn up," J whispered back.

J then went to the edge of the roof laying on his stomach to see if the cops were still in the house. I went to join him. He quickly tried to stop me from seeing, but he couldn't stop me in time.

I looked over the ledge of the roof and saw the cops dragging a very limp Doran out to a police van. His legs were loosely dangling beneath him. My heart cried out in agony as I quietly watched. Then for an instant Doran's eyes met mine. They looked at me assuringly as if Doran knew something that I didn't.

Doran and I always had such a close connection that we didn't need words to communicate. He would always call it the power of black love. I felt that love in that moment and I knew just what Doran was telling me. He was telling me not to worry. Though looking in my eyes he also knew that I would never do that.

Instantly, I visualized myself snuggled up on Doran's chest on a Sunday morning. I let all the other emotions go and allowed the feeling of love in that moment consume me.

Meanwhile, as the cop threw Doran into the van I heard him again scream out in pain. It looked like they had broken both of his legs as they were both quite contorted.

I kept my focus on my love for Doran. Suddenly, I felt that familiar feeling of lightness. I looked to the side of me and saw that my wings had returned. I looked below me and saw that I was levitating. I maintained my focus on love.

One cop jumped into the back of the van with Doran while the other closed the rear door of the van and then headed towards the driver's side with the key in hand.

I kept focusing. What happened next blew my human mind.

26

Beyond the control of my human mind I returned, my wings spread wide and I took flight. With a hunger for flesh I began to circle. It felt as if I hadn't eaten in thousands of years. My sense of smell was instantly heightened and the stench of nearby sick, wounded and weakened prey was intoxicating. My predatory instincts had taken control as I flew high, circling drunk with the thought feeding.

Then as if it was a magnetic pull I swooped down and grabbed the cop just as he was about to shut the door on the driver's side of the police van. I swiftly yanked him out of the van just barely within seconds of him shutting the door. The thrill of the hunt had by then heightened the intensity of my anticipation to feed and I had instantly become the ultimate predator.

Then, suddenly another urge overshadowed my anticipation. As I circled the van with the screaming cop tightly clutched in my talons I felt a familiar stare that drew me in.

It was Doran, but he was neither the white Doran nor the black one. He was an ibis-headed Doran standing upright with fully healed legs holding a staff burrowed deep into the heart of the other cop as he gazed at me in awe.

We locked eyes and I descended down to where he was using the cop, who was still tightly clutched by my talon, as my landing pad.

Doran and I looked at one another intensely and within moments we had resumed our white physical forms. Even in that form Doran's legs seemed fully healed as we both stood at the rear of the van still in shock.

I jumped off of the dead cop and ran up to Doran hugging him tightly and showering him with kisses.

"What was that?" he asked excitedly.

"It was black love baby!" I exclaimed still holding him tightly.

"Ha ha! Well that was some serious love! If I ever had any question about your love for me before it's damn sure gone now!" he gleamed.

"Oh yeah.... well I can say the same. You were loving me pretty good yourself from what I could see," I replied.

"I guess love truly does conquer all," Doran said.

Then J and Ina came running from out of the house and Ina ran up and gave Doran and I a huge hug. J stood still in a daze no doubt questioning if what he just witnessed was real.

Then going to hug us both he looked at Doran and said, "Man what the hell was that? I thought for sure we had lost you. It was hard as hell just to watch that, but I remembered what you said about doing things the right way in the right time."

"I know son and I'm proud of your because to tell you the truth I don't know that I could have done that and we both may have gotten killed," Doran said.

"Baby who were you and how did you make yourself shif?" I inquired.

"I can't even really explain it. It just seemed like an intense feeling of love overcame me and it was the only thing that I could think of. It was a feeling even stronger than the pain I was in. Next thing I knew I felt this feeling of lightness, like what we felt briefly when had all transformed at once. Then, I became this sort of half bird, half human thing. Once that happened something else took over and I was no longer in control of my actions...." Doran explained before I interrupted.

"Actually babe you were in control. The real you was in control. It was the evolved you," I corrected.

"You know you're right baby. That's actually exactly what it felt like. Then it started to get really hot and I had this intense hunger for flesh. It seemed to consume me. So I took the stake that instantly appeared in my hand and put it through the cop's heart. By then you came down and we turned back into these bodies.

"Wow dad! That's amazing! I'm so glad you figured it out," Ina squealed hugging Doran again.

"What do you mean figured it out baby? Figured what out?" Doran inquired.

"*Love* dad! The key to evolving is love. Once you and mom figured it out you could use your power to change into the bird! That's the same thing that happened on an episode of White Oblivion. The lady was gonna lose her man to the monster, but then she remembered how much she loved him and didn't want him to die and that's when she turned into the woman superhero and he turned into the man superhero," Ina said matter-of-factly.

We all looked at one another in puzzlement then Doran grabbed Ina's hand and said, "Ok let's go inside and discuss this show further cause I gotta know how this kid show is predicting everything."

We all nodded in agreement then filed into the house. When we got into the house the first thing that Doran did was secure the front door, putting on all the locks. We still hadn't figured out how they identified us as being a threat in the first place and before we discussed the cartoon we had to figure that out. For all we knew there were more cops on the way.

27

Just as that thought entered my mind Doran gestured for each of us to to pretend like he had been taken.

So J and I started a fake discussion carrying on the discussion as if Doran wasn't there. I figured Doran must have assumed that since they viewed him as a threat the house may have been bugged.

That did make me wonder how they even identified our family as being a threat. It seemed that Doran read my mind because as J and I talked Doran was busy taking extra precautions to secure the house and locate the bugs, if there were in fact any.

I figured it was probably happening to all the families. They were getting more fearful of an uprising and were starting to try to protect themselves. Thinking about it all made me sigh heavily. It was all a big mess.

Where were they taking everyone? And were they just going around rounding us all up? What were they planning to do?

Just then the thought popped into my mind that J was right. They knew who we were. They knew exactly who we were. It was just what the man who rammed his car into the Johnson's house was expressing when he said, "I know who you are!"

It *was* over for them and they know it which is why they were doing what they were doing, trying to buy time. They figured that taking some of us captive would buy them some time. But it wasn't gonna work I thought to myself.

I went to whisper all of this to J and Doran. They looked at me in agreement. This all made me wonder about Connie and this whole thing with her authorship of the cartoon.

White Oblivion was a very popular cartoon, which meant that she had to work *with* them to get it onto a major network. Then I had just remembered something. The night we went to the workshop Connie was not herself. She seemed to be holding something back. Besides that, that was the shortest lecture I'd ever heard.

Whispering to the two of them I said, "You know that workshop that Doran and I went to where Connie was presenting?" I asked.

They both shook their head signaling a yes waiting to hear where I was going with it.

"Well Connie said that she had travelled all over the world and saw this happening everywhere. But she wasn't very informative and considering how spooked out we all were she was actually quite short with us. Then the whole thing about the authorities looking for her since this hit the general population," I explained.

They both shrugged.

"It all makes sense. Connie was the Trojan Horse so to speak. She was who they used to identify us and when I say us I mean those of us who were ready to evolve. That's how they located us so quickly. There must be something more to who we truly are than even we know. I bet you it's been those of us that attended that workshop who have been the ones among the blacks who have been coming up 'missing,'" I explained further.

Doran nodded his head in agreement. Then Doran whispered that when he and J had gone out to retrieve empty bottles they'd heard some talk about that, but hadn't actually made the connection to the workshop.

Suddenly, just as we were putting more of the pieces together it started to heat up again. We all looked at each other and shrugged.

"It's getting hot again mom? Do you feel it?" Ina asked.

"I do feel it baby. I don't know what that's about. I wonder if it's heating up everywhere. Let's open the window to find out," I said heading toward a window in the kitchen room on the back side of the house to remain discreet. We didn't know if anyone was still watching the house or not. I opened the window and stuck my hand out and it felt like mid July outside. It had to be at least 90 degrees outside.

"Wow, it's hot as hell out there. What's going on?" I said thinking out loud.

"I wonder what's causing it. I'm thinking we should check online on some social media sites. I'm sure people are capturing this on film. Maybe we'll also see something that'll give us an idea as to where they're taking everybody," J offered going to retrieve his tablet.

While J looked into things I thought about how they must have been torturing the others.

Interrupting my thoughts J whispered, "I got something!"

Anxiously running over to J who was sitting on the couch on his tablet I asked, "Whatcha got?"

"I found several videos showing this same location. Look here's a really good one. Looks like this person is on the inside posting. I guess they didn't find his phone," J said showing me a clip of what looked like slave quarters in the middle of DC. As I watched I felt like I was time traveling. Had we gone back in time? I thought we were so past all of this savage behavior. I couldn't believe my eyes. Their paranoia was absurd. Surely, they knew that it would backfire as it always had.

"We have to do something. Besides that I think it has something to do with things heating up," J said.

"Yeah but we can't go up against them. I can only imagine how heavily guarded it is...." I said before the strangest thing happened.

I looked up and saw that Ina then J were levitating. They even had the same glow that I had when I was levitating. Also, like me they had shape-shifted into another being. Ina had taken on a cat-like face and J took on birdlike features similar to Doran's, the difference being that J looked like a hawk.

As I watched them in awe it began to get even hotter. Then I too began to levitate and transform. I looked and my wings had returned along with my beautiful brown skin, which I was so happy to see. Soon Doran transformed too.

"What is happening to us mom?" Ina asked with a puzzled expression, which quickly transformed into a smile. "This is great mom! It's just like on "White Oblivion."

"What do you mean by that Ina?" both Doran and I asked simultaneously.

"Well on White Oblivion after the special people changed they started to get powers and their bodies changed, well sort of," Ina explained.

"What do you mean by sort of?" I inquired.

"Well their bodies were never real in the first place so when they changed they realized that the mean people had put them in a dream world and they had been there so long they forgot they were dreaming. But then they started to remember and when they did their powers came back," Ina said matter-of-factly.

"Wow looks like Connie put it all in that cartoon. But why would she do all that then snitch on us? I doesn't make sense," I pondered aloud.

"Yeah but if what Ina says is true none of it even matters because no matter what they do to try to stop the change from happening the change is gonna happen regardless. If these bodies aren't real then neither is this place and neither are they. I say we go help the others now, while we're in this form. We don't know if it'll last. Besides that they're gonna start getting more and more desperate. Plus, we need to find out why things are heating up so much and what the connection is between the heat and what's happening. That's the one thing we can't seem to explain.

"You won't get any argument here, but how do we all get around in this form and stay together? I did it before, but I don't know if I can do it again and sustain it," I pointed out.

Before J could respond I was distracted by Doran who began to look a little weird. He appeared to be his evolved self, but something was off. He had a reddish glow and moments later so did J.

28

Looking at Doran and J strangely I asked, "Guys what's happening to you?"

With a mixed look of joy and grief Doran looked at me and said, "Opportunity. Baby we have to go and we have to go now, but you and Ina need to stay here. The others need our help. You're right. They are being tortured, but not even the worst of their torturing attempts can hurt these bodies. That's why we have to go now. It's time to end this for good. I think that's what's heating things up," Doran explained.

"Yeah but how are we gonna get back together? Are you gonna come back for us?" I asked.

"I promise you I will baby. We will definitely get back together," Doran said reassuringly.

I knew Doran was just telling me what I wanted to hear. The truth was he didn't know how things would turn out. I got a bad feeling in the pit of my stomach. I knew that things were about to get worse and that there was a strong possibility that Ina and I would never see Doran or J again. I knew that in this whole thing there would be sacrifices, but I didn't want that to be the two most important men in my life!

Just then we heard yelling and screaming in the streets outside. I floated to the window and saw people fighting one another and some had the same reddish glow that Doran and J had.

Immediately I turned around and they were gone! I had a feeling that they were being influenced by this wave of heat that seemed to be infecting many of the people that I saw fighting in the streets.

It was just like Connie had said. People were regressing. They were fighting back in ways that just weren't helping us. In fact, it was making things worse. The worse part was that Doran and J had now become part of the regression.

Then I remembered what Doran himself had said, which was that that was the plan all along. The plan was to provoke us to act this way, knowing that it would make us regress.

Things were getting way out of hand and something had to be done to stop it. Balance had to be restored.

Ina looked at me saddened by the sudden departure of Doran and J and said, "What now? How do we get them back mom? We have to get them back!"

She was riddled with worry as was I. I tried to think of some comforting words but came up empty. I didn't know what to say. I didn't even know what to think about what was to come.

Then my thoughts unexpectedly shifted to Connie and why she played the role that she played in all of this. I couldn't decide if Connie was friend or foe. Yet the more I thought about it I was convinced that she was playing for the other team, working against her own. Though I couldn't for the life of me imagine why she would align herself with the losing team. After all, they weren't even real and she knew it. Then I considered that perhaps she was just playing like she was helping them.

I just couldn't resolve what her angle was. I couldn't figure her out. I couldn't understand why she played such a big part in everything that had happened. It seemed at every turn her name just kept coming up.

As I pondered such thoughts we heard a huge boom! It sounded like an atomic bomb. Moments later the air was filled with smoke and we saw that it *was* some type of bomb. Ina and I went back to the window to see what was happening. We saw a band of white kids, who we couldn't identify as actual whites or blacks in white skinsuits. They were riding through the streets in tanks standing at the top and yelling out obscenities. Some ran around terrorizing the neighborhood yelling that it was time to rid the world of the white devils and that their time had come. They were sick of their oppression and now it was time for them to pay. It looked like a scene from the movie *The Purge*. After hearing their protests it was clear who they were and it was a definite sign that we were in fact regressing.

While I totally agreed with everything that they said I didn't agree with their methods. We finally had a way out of the prison that had become our life and they ruining it.

We watched them go into some of the homes of our white neighbors dragging some of them out and torturing them the same way that I'd watched Doran being tortured. As I watched I couldn't help but feel vindicated. At the same time, the instant I did I descended back into my white body as had Ina. It was as if we were all linked to the boys terrorizing our neighborhood.

Then I felt the most intense feeling of anger brewing inside of me as I began to get hotter and hotter. It became unbearably hot and I noticed that Ina was experiencing the same thing In fact, we were both starting to take on the same reddish glow that Doran, J and the others had.

Quickly, remembering what Connie said I willed myself to control my emotions. I refused to let the anger consume me.

"Don't let it consume you Ina. Stay neutral. That's the key. This doesn't have to control us. Go numb! Do it now!" I insisted.

Looking at me Ina obeyed. As I looked at her I saw her switch back and forth from white to her cat form. From the look on her face she seemed to be witnessing me doing the same thing.

It was as though there was an internal struggle going on within us as we tried to resolve whether or not we would maintain control over our emotion or let them control us giving into the anger.

As justified as our anger was for all that we'd endured as a people it simply wasn't serving us. I noticed the more we were able to control our emotions, the more we were able to control our physical form.

Then within moments we started to levitate again and take on our evolved form.

"We did it mom!" Ina gleamed.

"Yes we did baby!" I replied.

Hoping that we all had shifted back I started to feel better until I looked out the window and saw that the boys on the tanks had shifted back into his lower form. They had a very pale white, almost alien appearance.

I glided out the window and said to them, "You have to try harder. Don't let it control you," I pled.

Walking towards me one of them replied, "That's easy for you to say. You haven't been through what we've been through. We deserve some justice and finally we can get some. We ain't goin nowhere until we do."

"That's just it though. Without peace there is no justice. Don't become them. Nothing about them is just. Embrace your peace and you'll get all the justice and vindication you need. I promise you will. I know it's been hard for you. It's been hard for all of us. But if you let the anger go you'll see that you possess a power that will take us far beyond the confines of this place," I said convincingly.

"I love you and that all sounds good, but right now what will feel good is some get back. You two will never understand what we had to endure. I'll be back," the young boy said.

Just then I recognized him. It was J! Then the moment he saw that I recognized him he was gone.

I couldn't believe it. Just like that my son was gone. Ina was crying hysterically. I was so distraught I didn't have the will to comfort her. I had lost the two most important men in my life and felt like there was nothing I could do about it..

29

My mind was racing. I refused to lose my men to mere emotion. I had to figure out a way to get them back. They were running around like sociopaths whose humanity switch was completely turned off.

Because I was so connected to Doran I could feel his anger welling up inside of me. I had to break the hold that it had over them. Quickly I thought of what Connie had said. So I asked Ina if anything like what was happening had happened in the cartoon.

She informed me that there was an episode where such a thing had happened. She said when it happened the world was destroyed and all of the people descended into lower forms. A new world was then created that was like a perpetual warzone.

I refused to accept that's how things would end in our case. Immediately I grabbed ahold of Ina's hands, closed my eyes and instructed her to do the same. We both focused on assuming our evolved form, powers and all. After several attempts we had done it! We were not only levitating, but we both felt a powerful force welling up inside of us.

That was progress, but I was determined to go a step further. We needed to tap into some serious powers. We needed to make some things happen this time.

Ina and I focused some more with everything that we had in us. As we did we felt lighter and lighter. The lighter we became the brighter our bodies lit up and we began to easily manipulate our bodies. I looked into Ina's eyes and they were more cat-like than ever. In the meantime, we kept getting hotter and hotter until the air was too hot to breathe.

Then, as we looked around we began to see others around us. Like us they were all brightly lit. They all began to take the forms of other ancient beings. Some of them assumed forms for which there was no description.

Then we all seemed to automatically bind together. Simultaneously, we began to remember who we were. Not only that, we could see what we each came to do as was evident in the form assumed.

Instinctively we looked into one another's eyes and through them we could see the reflection of our true self. Looking into Ina's eyes I was an ancient vulture goddess who had come to purify the world and restore balance. The instant this revelation came to me my wings took flight. I must have flown to the ends of the planet's skies because I could see everything. Ina, a stunning lion goddess, lept up to where I was and looked into my eyes seeing her own reflection and the most astounding revelation of all. Ina had, like me, come to purify the world, but through fire and the time had come for her to do just that.

Once all the others had seen their true identities having what felt like one consciousness we each lent Ina and others like her our power. The more we connected and focused, the hotter it became. It was so hot that it felt as though there would be an explosion. In fact, had we been in our previous physical form we probably would have exploded.

Moments later our eyes began to glow and in them shown the ends of a millions of lifetimes. I looked at Ina the others like her and they looked like a pride of lions made of fire. They smiled and their grin sent screams piercing into oblivion. It was the screams of what seemed to be a billion generations of souls.

Then we began to feel their fear. We felt it in the form of an excruciating pain that pierced every fiber, every cell and every atom in our being.

Through our glowing eyes we saw the barbaric means of torture and oppression that we had for millions of years withstood. Then we felt our will to survive break through transforming into a torch. It was a torch of justice, balance and peace. In our glowing eyes we saw and recognized ourselves as the ancient ones, the gods, goddesses, Titans, dark terrestrials, the chosen ones and we were there for the end of days, the final destruction of the parasitic rule.

Soon the other vulture goddesses and I gathered into a circle wing to wing. In the center we conjured a horrific monstrous being waiting to feed. With a glance we extracted the parasites from the world. Then we fed them to the monstrous being.

Once we did the world heated up to the point that, like bedbugs, it began to explode. Simultaneously, we began to come into our light bodies. The hotter we got, the lighter we felt. Then we felt a weightlessness. We were no longer weighed down by our emotions. Our pains no longer deluded us. Our fear no longer paralyzed us and our anger no longer held us captive. We were in the midst of our ascent and what was once white oblivion quickly began to fade away.

Within moments there was a thick, black midst. Through it we were unable to see one another, but our ability to sense one another was stronger than ever. We were more connected than we ever had been.

Then there was silence for some time and before long the midst began to clear. We all opened our eyes to find that we had all transformed into vultures and instantly we all flew. Together we flew for eons. Using the ethers as our transport we glided looking at the mountains of corpses that lie beneath us.

As a group we descended and ate together feeding off of the carcasses of the fallen ones. Then after several days of feasting we saw that the world was again purified.

Yet it was not the old world. It was a new world in which we put much care into creating.

We had learned much from our mistakes and so the new world was all that we had dreamed of. It was the kind of world that we had prior to then only thought existed in dreams. Once we realized our power to make our dreams come true the new world simply came into being, just like that!

The next day the sun shined bright. All was quiet, peaceful and just. Parasites existed, but in their rightful place. Many of us had taken on semi-human forms and I was one among them. The difference was that we were no longer bound by these forms and could transform at will.

I had again taken the form of a feminine being and had settled in a small cottage in a village off the coast of the most beautiful ocean. The waters were a clear lavender that sparkled against the light of the stars.

Other among us had chosen to be stars and the way the light from the stars sparkled on the water created the most breath-taking views.

I had come outside to enjoy the warmth of the midday starlight when the most attractive guy approached my porch. He was so familiar to me, but I couldn't put my finger on where I knew him from.

As I tried to recall he walked up to my porch and looked at me with the most gorgeous smile and said, "Hello again goddess! It's a pleasant surprise seeing you again!"

Instantly my heart fluttered, I smiled, ran up to him and planted a big kiss on his soft, full, chocolate-coated lips. As I released him I saw the most beautiful little girl waiting patiently behind him and beside her was the most handsome young man. They both ran up to me and we all hugged each other tightly forming an unbreakable bond of pure love. There we remained on planet Black Oblivion.

If you enjoyed this book or received value from it in any way, then I'd like to ask you for a favor. Would you be kind enough to leave a review for this book on Amazon? It'd be greatly appreciated!

About the Author....

Amirah Bellamy is the Board Chair of Life Arts Institute. She is an artist of many crafts. She's been a writer for over 19 years, a yogi for over 9 years, a singer for over 15 years, nutritionista for over 16 years and has thoroughly enjoyed being mom to 2 beautiful children.

To learn more about Amirah Bellamy

email.... amirahbellamy@gmail.com
or
visit..... www.EthericRealmsInv.com

Other books by this author also available (Visit www.EthericRealmsInv.com to learn more!) ....